# *Contents*

**PAPER 1: EXPLORATIONS IN CREATIVE READING AND WRITING**

**PAPER 2: WRITERS' VIEWPOINTS AND PERSPECTIVES**

Please note: this book is not endorsed by or affiliated to any exam boards; I am simply an experienced teacher using my expertise to help students.

# Introduction

This guide was written by Andrew Bruff who, in 2011, had a vision to share his GCSE expertise in English language and literature. This resulted in his first online tutorial video at http://youtube.com/mrbruff.

Seven years later, his videos have been viewed over 50 million times across 214 different nations. To accompany these videos, he has published over 20 revision guides, many of which are best sellers. His guides to the previous GCSEs in English language and literature topped the list of Amazon best sellers for over 45 weeks and achieved huge acclaim.

This guide to the AQA GCSE English language exams aims to build on those strengths. It contains detailed help on every question in the exams. Please note that this book is not endorsed by or affiliated to any exam boards; Mr Bruff is simply an experienced teacher using his expertise to help students.

Follow Mr Bruff on Twitter @MrBruffEnglish or visit his website www.mrbruff.com for details of his range of GCSE and A level revision guides.

**FREE GIFT**: The ebook edition of this book contains colour images and links to five exclusive videos. You deserve those too, so email info@mrbruff.com with proof of purchase, and he will email you the ebook edition for free.

## Dedication

Mr Bruff would like to thank a number of people who have been instrumental in supporting his work:

- Sunny Ratilal and Sam Perkins, who worked on the front cover design.
- Noah and Elijah, who lost their 'daddy' to the office far too many times in the completion of this book.
- Peter Tobin, Kerry Lewis and Georgie Bottomley—three integral members of the mrbruff.com team. Their behind-the-scenes work enables him to keep up the 'front of house': thank you!
- Claire, his lovely wife, who got behind him in his vision and supports him in it every day.
- Chris Bruff—a brother who has put his money where his mouth is and supported the work that benefits so many.

## A word from our sponsors:

Developed by leading experts, the **ChatterStars** app uses question styles which target **rapid vocabulary acquisition**, through kinaesthetic use of repetition, image, sound and reward. Our innovative question styles link to vocabulary development stages and are aligned to the **national curriculum**, providing schools and parents with a go-to resource to secure rapid progress.

Uniquely, the **ChatterStars** app will provide a **vocabulary-age**, enabling schools and parents to track progress. Matching questions to a child's needs, teachers and parents can be confident their children are learning exactly what they need to learn - perfect for **KS2 SATs**, **11+ exams** and **GCSE**, improving **expression**, **comprehension** and **writing** for all pupils aged 6-16, across all areas!

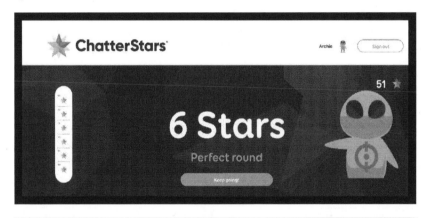

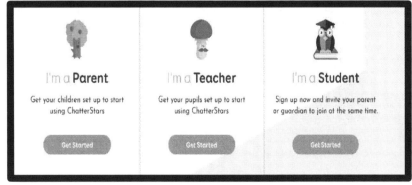

- Follow us - Chatterstars: the vocab app
- www.chatterstars.co.uk
- Download the app: app store and Google Play

3

# PAPER 1: EXPLORATIONS IN CREATIVE READING AND WRITING

## SECTION A: CREATIVE READING

## Overview

Section A of paper 1 focuses on what is called 'creative reading'. In this section of the exam, you will be presented with an extract from a novel or short story from the twentieth or twenty-first century. It is an unseen extract, meaning you will almost certainly never have seen it before. You might get lucky and be presented with something you've once read, but the chances of that happening are slim. The extract will be approximately 40-50 lines in length. It will be taken from a key point in a text: perhaps the opening or a moment of extreme tension. The purpose of Section A is to consider how the writer uses descriptive and narrative techniques to capture the interest of the reader.

There are millions of works of fiction out there for you to read. The variety of genres and forms available is overwhelming, yet all have one thing in common: their authors want the reader to find them interesting. Successful writers use a wide range of devices to engage the interest of a reader. Section A will test your ability to spot these devices.

Section A contains four questions: you must answer all of them. The first question is a short question worth 4 marks whereas questions 2 and 3 are longer questions worth 8 marks each, and question 4 is an extended question worth 20 marks. This question structure (moving from easy to hard) is intended to help you 'warm up' with the easier opening questions. This prepares you to tackle the bigger challenges later in the paper. Because of this, I always recommend attempting the paper in chronological order, answering the questions in order.

Section A assesses three different assessment objectives: AO1, AO2 and AO4. A successful student will always know which assessment objectives are being tested in each question. It's essential that you become very familiar with those objectives, so let's look at them:

| |
|---|
| AO1: Identify and interpret explicit and implicit information and ideas. Select and synthesise evidence from different texts |
| AO2: Explain, comment on and analyse how writers use language and structure to achieve effects and influence readers, using relevant subject terminology to support your views |
| AO3: Compare writers' ideas and perspectives, as well as how these are conveyed across two or more texts |
| AO4: Evaluate texts critically, and support this with appropriate textual references |

*This table contains public sector information licensed under the Open Government Licence v3.0.*

At the start of the exam, you will receive your question paper and an insert to read. For this section of the guide, we shall use an extract from Mary Shelley's 'Frankenstein'.

# Source A

*This extract is taken from the middle of a novel by Mary Shelley. In this section, Frankenstein, a scientist, finally finds success in creating life from body parts of the dead.*

1    It was on a dreary night of November that I beheld the accomplishment of my toils. With an anxiety that almost amounted to agony, collected the instruments of life around me, that I might infuse a spark of being into the lifeless thing that lay at my feet. It was already one in the morning; the rain pattered dismally against the panes, and my candle was nearly burnt

5    out, when, by the glimmer of the half-extinguished light, I saw the dull yellow eye of the creature open; it breathed hard, and a convulsive motion agitated its limbs.

How can I describe my emotions at this catastrophe, or how delineate the wretch whom with such infinite pains and care I had endeavoured to form? His limbs were in proportion, and I had selected his features as beautiful. Beautiful! -- Great God! His yellow skin scarcely

10    covered the work of muscles and arteries beneath; his hair was of a lustrous black, and flowing; his teeth of a pearly whiteness; but these luxuriances only formed a more horrid contrast with his watery eyes, that seemed almost of the same colour as the dun white sockets in which they were set, his shrivelled complexion and straight black lips.

The different accidents of life are not so changeable as the feelings of human nature. I had

15    worked hard for nearly two years, for the sole purpose of infusing life into an inanimate body. For this I had deprived myself of rest and health. I had desired it with an ardour that far exceeded moderation; but now that I had finished, the beauty of the dream vanished, and breathless horror and disgust filled my heart. Unable to endure the aspect of the being I had created, I rushed out of the room, continued a long time traversing my bed chamber,

20    unable to compose my mind to sleep. At length lassitude succeeded to the tumult I had before endured; and I threw myself on the bed in my clothes, endeavouring to seek a few moments of forgetfulness. But it was in vain; I slept, indeed, but I was disturbed by the wildest dreams. I thought I saw Elizabeth, in the bloom of health, walking in the streets of Ingolstadt. Delighted and surprised, I embraced her; but as I imprinted the first kiss on her

25    lips, they became livid with the hue of death; her features appeared to change, and I thought that I held the corpse of my dead mother in my arms; a shroud enveloped her form, and I saw the grave-worms crawling in the folds of the flannel. I started from my sleep with horror; a cold dew covered my forehead, my teeth chattered, and every limb became convulsed: when, by the dim and yellow light of the moon, as it forced its way through the

30    window shutters, I beheld the wretch -- the miserable monster whom I had created. He held up the curtain of the bed and his eyes, if eyes they may be called, were fixed on me. His jaws opened, and he muttered some inarticulate sounds, while a grin wrinkled his cheeks. He might have spoken, but I did not hear; one hand was stretched out, seemingly to detain me, but I escaped, and rushed down stairs. I took refuge in the courtyard belonging to the house which I inhabited; where I remained during the rest of the night, walking up and down in the greatest agitation, listening attentively, catching and fearing each sound as if it

were to announce the approach of the demoniacal corpse to which I had so miserably given life.

**TOP TIP:** You might think this extract is quite complex, and you'd be right. Prepare for this by reading extracts from a range of texts. A simple suggestion is to read the opening page of any fiction book and ask yourself, *What has the writer done to make the reader want to read on?*

## *QUESTION 1*

Question 1 is the exam board's 'easy opener', which intends to warm you up. This question asks you to list **four things** you learn from a specific part of the extract, and is worth 4 marks. The exam board does not make any recommendations on timing, but it is fairly easy to make some rough calculations:

The exam is 1 hr, 45 minutes in length (105 minutes). There are 80 marks available in the entire paper. If we allow 10 minutes to read the insert, that leaves you with around 95 minutes in which to achieve 80 marks. With that in mind, you should aim to spend around 1-1.5 minutes per mark available.

Question 1 should take you around 5 minutes. It is assessing the first part of AO1:

- Identify and interpret explicit and implicit information and ideas

So, what does that mean in simple language? Well, it means that you can read the extract and understand it, both the obvious bits and the subtler hidden meanings.

Let's look at an example. Question 1 will direct you to specific lines from which to find your answer. So, if it says 'read lines 7-13', you must base your answer only on the lines identified in the question. Remember: this is the start of the exam. With those exam nerves, it's easy to miss this crucial direction to line references, but you have to make sure that you take your answers from the correct lines. The lines will be numbered on the left-hand side of the page, but it is very easy in the stress of an exam to totally ignore this and to take your answer from somewhere else in the text. My advice is to draw around the lines to make sure you know where your answer needs to come from.

Once you've identified the lines from which you need to find your answer, the next step is to look carefully at the topic of the question. Question 1 will ask you about a certain topic, e.g. the weather. Once again, there is potential to make a mistake here: you need to write about the topic of the question. If the question is about the weather, write about the weather. Don't broaden your comments to a wider topic such as 'setting'. Again, it sounds simple, but anything can go wrong in the exam.

Now for some good news: quoting or paraphrasing is acceptable. That means you can use the exact wording from the text as part of your answer (as long as the quotation is answering the question). This is great news, considering you only want to spend 5 minutes on this question. Remember that question 1 is worth the least marks in the whole paper, so stick to the timings: spend a maximum of 5 minutes on it!

Let's look at a sample question:

---

**Question 1**

Read lines 7-13.
List four things from this part of the text about Frankenstein's creature.

**[4 marks]**

A.

B.

C.

D.

---

**NOTE:** There are a few things to be careful of here. Firstly, you need to take your answers from between lines 7-13. So, even if you find out things about Frankenstein's creature in line 14, you can't include this information in your answer. The second point to be aware of is that this question is about Frankenstein's creature, not Frankenstein himself.

Remember that you can take a direct quote from the text and use it as your answer. Here's a response that's worth full marks:

---

**SAMPLE ANSWER**

A. His skin was yellow.
B. His hair was black.
C. His teeth were white.
D. His eyes were watery.

---

As you can see, this is a simple question. There are really only two ways you can go wrong with question 1:

1. You don't choose your points from the lines referenced.

2. You don't choose points that answer the question i.e. 'about Frankenstein's creature'.

Although this question may seem simple, it will reward you with 4 marks that you don't then need to scrape back later in the paper. Achieving full marks in this easy question means you don't have so much pressure on yourself for the trickier ones later in the exam.

# QUESTION 2

Question 2 is based around another section of the same text.

This question assesses the language element of AO2: 'Explain, comment on and analyse how different writers use language and structure to achieve effects and influence readers, using relevant subject terminology to support their views'.

So, what do we mean when we refer to language analysis? Put simply, we mean to investigate a writer's use of words, language features and sentence forms. You are looking for occasions where it seems that the writer has deliberately used these to achieve a specific effect on the reader. If that sounds confusing, don't worry–we'll look at an example.

Question 2 is worth 8 marks, and you should spend around 10 minutes on it. Here's a sample question:

---

**Question 2**

Take a detailed look at lines 1-6 of the source:

*It was on a dreary night of November that I beheld the accomplishment of my toils. With an anxiety that almost amounted to agony, I collected the instruments of life around me, that I might infuse a spark of being into the lifeless thing that lay at my feet. It was already one in the morning; the rain pattered dismally against the panes, and my candle was nearly burnt out, when, by the glimmer of the half-extinguished light, I saw the dull yellow eye of the creature open; it breathed hard, and a convulsive motion agitated its limbs.*

How does the writer use language to describe the weather?

You could write about:

- Individual words and phrases
- Language features and techniques
- Sentence forms

[8 marks]

---

To achieve full marks, you need to write answers that are perceptive. 'Perceptive' basically means thinking beyond the obvious. Remember, examiners mark hundreds of papers and will read hundreds of responses to the same question. If you are to achieve top marks, you want to be making points that most other students do not make.

The bullet points in this question serve as a useful reminder of the kinds of things you can write about. However, in the November 2018 exam, the extract had no sentence forms worthy of analysis, so don't panic if you feel you can't cover all three areas in your answer.

Before you look at the sample answer, re-read the extract and think about which language features you might analyse. Remember, the question is about the description of weather, so any language used to describe characters is not important here.

Let's look at the three bullet points in detail, starting with individual words and phrases.

## INDIVIDUAL WORDS AND PHRASES

You need to avoid writing about vague, generalised effects in your answer to question 2. If you write things like 'this makes the reader want to read on', you will fail to achieve high marks. You need to avoid comments that could be applied to ANY text by making your comments specific to the text that you are reading.

So how do you avoid these generalised comments? The best thing to do is this: read the extract and ask yourself, *What is the desired effect the writer is aiming to achieve in this extract?* It could be a sense of boredom, energy, danger, threat, humour, etc. Choose the desired effect, and THEN look for the language uses that achieve this effect. This will help you to focus your analysis and avoid vague comments.

NOTE: The effect does not always have to be emotive. Be specific in your analysis.

Once you have a clear idea of the effect the writer wishes to achieve, you can scan the extract for words or phrases which achieve that effect. In our example, the weather is described in such negative terms, creating a sense of danger or threat, so you might like to pick words which create this effect:

'dreary'
'night', 'November'
'pattered'
'dismally'

---

**SAMPLE ANSWER 1**

Shelley uses a wide range of negative language to describe the weather. To begin with, the rain not only falls, but it patters 'dismally'. This is a very negative word that creates the feeling that something bad is going to happen. Similarly, the night is described with the adjective 'dreary'. These words create a sense of danger.

---

OK, that paragraph was adequate, but it certainly wasn't perceptive. The more perceptive points are likely to come from looking at language features and sentence forms. Let's now look at language features.

## LANGUAGE FEATURES

As this question is based on a literary extract and not a piece of non-fiction, the language features we should look out for are examples of figurative language.

Figurative language is where a writer goes beyond the literal meaning of a word or phrase. You will probably be familiar with many of these examples from your work on poetry analysis. Although it is tempting to create an acronym that covers a few of the key examples, it will be much more useful for you to learn them all:

**Alliteration**: Repetition of the same sound at the beginning of words. For example: *The man moved mountains.*

**Assonance:** Repetition of vowel sounds in words that start with different consonants. For example: *Light the fire up high.*

**Consonance:** Repetition of consonant sounds in words which are close together in a sentence. For example: *I think I thanked the wrong uncle.*

**Note:** remember, consonance is repetition of sounds, not necessarily letters. Consonance is often a tricky device to spot, because the repetition does not have to occur at the beginning of the word (that's alliteration). For example,: *Matt picked up the ticket.*

**Euphemism:** An indirect or mild word/phrase used to replace one that is thought to be too harsh or offensive. For example*: I'm going to have to let you go* (instead of *sack you*).

**Hyperbole:** Deliberate exaggeration for effect. For example: *I've told you a million times, no Xbox after 10pm!*

**Idiom:** An expression that holds a different meaning to its literal meaning. For example: *Granddad kicked the bucket.* This idiom means 'died', and does not refer to any literal bucket kicking.

**Metaphor:** Describing something by stating that it is something else. For example: *He flew down the road in his car.* He did not literally fly, but the metaphor suggests the idea that he drove so fast that he achieved speeds like those of an aircraft.

Sometimes you will find a metaphor that is used throughout a piece of writing (or in this case, an extract). This is called an **extended metaphor**.

**Personification:** Giving human characteristics to something that is not human. For example: *The flames danced playfully in the fire.* Flames cannot dance–this is a human characteristic to describe the way the flames move around.

**Onomatopoeia:** Where the word imitates the sound of the thing it is naming. For example: *I saved my work with a click of the mouse.* When you say the word 'click', it makes the sound of a 'click'. Other examples are *splash, drip* and *bang.*

**Oxymoron:** Placing two words together which are opposite to each other. For example: *Act naturally, pretty ugly, jumbo shrimp.*

**Pun:** A joke about words that sound alike but they have different meanings. For example: *Santa's little helpers are called subordinate clauses.*

**Pathetic Fallacy:** The use of setting to reflect a character's mood. For example: 'The rain pattered dismally against the panes'. Here the rain reflects the mood of the narrator.

**Sibilance:** most commonly, the repetition of the soft *–s* and *–sh* sounds in words. This is like alliteration, but the sounds can be anywhere in a word. For example: *The silken sad uncertain rustling sound.*

**Simile:** Describing something by stating that it is like something else, using the word 'as' or 'like'. For example: *He was as cold as ice.* The difference between a simile and a metaphor is that a simile describes something as if it is *like* something else whereas a metaphor describes something as if it *is* something else.

**Symbolism:** Where one thing is meant to represent something else. For example, the colour black is often used to symbolise evil or death.

## ANALYSING LANGUAGE FEATURES

So, let's look for these features in the extract:

*It was on a dreary night of November that I beheld the accomplishment of my toils. With an anxiety that almost amounted to agony, I collected the instruments of life around me, that I might infuse a spark of being into the lifeless thing that lay at my feet. It was already one in the morning; the rain pattered dismally against the panes, and my candle was nearly burnt out, when, by the glimmer of the half-extinguished light, I saw the dull yellow eye of the creature open; it breathed hard, and a convulsive motion agitated its limbs.*

Here's what I spotted:

1. Pathetic fallacy: 'rain pattered dismally'
2. Onomatopoeia: 'pattered'

As you can see, these two points are more sophisticated than the simple language analysis from paragraph 1. However, it's not enough to simply identify the language features—you must explain the **effect** on the reader. This bit is the hardest bit. Put simply, you should ask yourself: why did the writer use that device? Does it make me feel a certain way? Does it make me think of a certain thing? Does it emphasise a certain point? The hard truth is that the effect depends on the context of the extract itself. Let's look at our two examples:

## 1. Pathetic fallacy: 'rain pattered dismally'

What is the effect of the fact that it is raining? How does this reflect Frankenstein's mood? We could argue that the grim weather reflects and foreshadows Frankenstein's mood over his creation. You can play around with different ideas when writing about pathetic fallacy—no single answer is the 'correct' answer. If you can explain your thinking, then anything is valid.

## 2. Onomatopoeia: 'pattered'

The use of onomatopoeia is very effective. By describing the sound made by the rain as it hits the window, the reader can imagine the scene more vividly—it's as if we too can hear the raindrops. This then scares the reader and increases the tension. We begin to experience the events of this chapter as if we are in the room with Frankenstein himself.

Let's put these points into a sample answer over the page:

As you can see, examining the writer's use of literary features allows us to produce a much more perceptive answer.

Thirdly, let's look at the writer's use of sentence forms. You can approach this in terms of sentence length, or if you're confident with grammar you might look for the different sentence types:

## SENTENCE FORMS

### Simple Sentences

Simple sentences contain a subject and a verb.

**Example:** *He laughed.*

In this example, we have a verb (in this case, an action): 'laughed'. If we ask ourselves who or what is 'doing' the verb, the answer is 'he'. Therefore, 'he' is the subject. Simple sentences are mostly, but not always, short.

It's possible to add adjectives and adverbs to simple sentences: *The tired old man walked slowly along the ancient stone path.* Although this sentence is longer, it still only contains one subject and one verb: 'man' and 'walked', so it is a simple sentence.

### Compound Sentences

Compound sentences join two independent clauses (that look like simple sentences) with one of the following words, called co-ordinating conjunctions:

**F**or
**A**nd
**N**or
**B**ut
**O**r
**Y**et
**S**o

You might have heard about them in school as 'FANBOYS'. (The conjunction 'for' is a slightly old-fashioned word, used to mean 'because'.)

We usually have a comma before these conjunctions.

**Example:** *The man laughed, and his wife cried.*

Here we have two independent clauses:

The man laughed (subject = man, verb = laughed)

His wife cried (subject = wife, verb = cried).

All we've done is join them together with one of the FANBOYS conjunctions and added a comma.


## Complex Sentences

Complex sentences have different (subordinating) conjunctions such as:

although
because
even if
if
while

**Example:** *I love you although you drive me crazy.*

If the subordinating conjunction is in the middle of the sentence, there is no comma. If the sentence starts with a subordinating conjunction, there is a comma:

**Example:** *Although you drive me crazy, I love you.*

Complex sentences can be divided into two parts:

1. The part which makes sense on its own. We call this the main clause and it looks like a simple sentence. In the above example, the main clause is 'I love you'.

2. The part which does not make sense on its own. We call this the subordinate clause. In the example above, the subordinate clause begins with the subordinating conjunction 'although you drive me crazy'.

The above is just one example of many different types of complex sentence.

## Compound-complex sentences

A compound-complex sentence consists of a compound sentence (two independent clauses joined with a FANBOYS, or co-ordinating, conjunction) and at least one subordinate clause.

**Example:** *I bought this book because it looked useful, but now I am confused.*

Let's break it down:

'I bought this book' = independent clause

'because it looked useful' = subordinate clause

'but' = FANBOYS (co-ordinating) conjunction

'now I am confused' = independent clause

## Minor sentences (or fragments)

A minor sentence, sometimes called a fragment, is a word, phrase or clause that does not have the grammar of the above sentences.

**Examples:** Yes, please! No pain, no gain. Hi!


## WHY IS IT IMPORTANT?

It's not enough just to identify the sentence types used in an extract. You need to think about **why** they are used. Probably the easiest way to do this is to think about sentence length. Writers often use very long sentences to create an overwhelming or depressing atmosphere. Very short sentences, in contrast, create a sense of energy, pace and panic. Why? Because long sentences are hard to read (overwhelming, you could say), and short sentences create pace as you are forced to take so many short breaths in time with the full stops. If you're a grammar whizz, you might be able to write about the sentence types that are employed (minor, simple, compound, complex or compound-complex). If not, just write about long and short sentences.

So, let's look back at the extract and consider the sentence types. Remember, we're just looking at the bits that describe the weather. See if you can work out the sentence types and spot where Shelley is using them for effect:

> *It was on a dreary night of November that I beheld the accomplishment of my toils. With an anxiety that almost amounted to agony, I collected the instruments of life around me, that I might infuse a spark of being into the lifeless thing that lay at my feet. It was already one in the morning; the rain pattered dismally against the panes, and my candle was nearly burnt out, when, by the glimmer of the half-extinguished light, I saw the dull yellow eye of the creature open; it breathed hard, and a convulsive motion agitated its limbs.*

How did you do? You hopefully spotted how the final sentence is a very long (and very confusing) sentence:

> *It was already one in the morning; the rain pattered dismally against the panes, and my candle was nearly burnt out, when, by the glimmer of the half-extinguished light, I saw the dull yellow eye of the creature open; it breathed hard, and a convulsive motion agitated its limbs.*

To see just how long this sentence is, try and read it aloud in one breath. Hard, isn't it?

**SAMPLE ANSWER 3**

Shelley uses sentence form to convey the overwhelming power of the bad weather in the extract. The long sentence 'It was already one in the morning...a convulsive motion agitated its limbs' is made up of numerous clauses and is so long that it is difficult to read aloud without becoming breathless. Shelley deliberately uses this technique to convey the fact that the weather is overwhelming, just like the use of sentence structure. With two semicolons and five commas, this sentence is chaotic. The chaotic sentence structure reflects the chaotic weather, mirroring the chaos of the experiment taking place.

**NOTE:** You'll see that I did not quote the whole sentence. To do so would take too many of my precious 10 minutes. If you're quoting a long section of the text, just quote the start and end, and place an ellipsis in the middle.

# QUESTION 3

While questions 1 and 2 are based on extracts, question 3 is based on the whole source. In theory, you should know the source quite well by now. You've read it once and answered two questions in detail about two sections. Now, you're going to write about the whole thing.

Question 3 assesses the structure element of AO2: Explain, comment on and analyse how different writers use language and structure to achieve effects and influence readers, using relevant subject terminology to support their views.

So, what do we mean by the term 'structure'? In simple terms, we are talking about how the text is organised. In other words, what happens where. Let's look at a typical question.

---

**Question 3**

Answer this question based on the whole source. This extract is taken from the middle of a novel.

How has the writer used structure to interest the reader?

You may write about:

      - What the writer focuses on at the start
      - How and why this focus changes through the extract
      - Other structural features

                                                **[8 marks]**

---

Once again, these bullet points are here to help you, so let's look at them one by one.

**WHAT THE WRITER FOCUSES ON AT THE START**

By 'start', let's examine the first paragraph of the extract on a sentence-by-sentence basis:

*It was on a dreary night of November that I beheld the accomplishment of my toils. With an anxiety that almost amounted to agony, I collected the instruments of life around me, that I might infuse a spark of being into the lifeless thing that lay at my feet. It was already one in the morning; the rain pattered dismally against the panes, and my candle was nearly burnt out, when, by the glimmer of the half-extinguished light, I saw the dull yellow eye of the creature open; it breathed hard, and a convulsive motion agitated its limbs.*

What do you notice about the structure of this paragraph? What happens where? One practical approach to this question is to think about what happens on a sentence-by-sentence basis. Here are some initial thoughts:

**Sentence 1:** *It was on a dreary night of November that I beheld the accomplishment of my toils.*

This first sentence begins by establishing the setting through time of day and month. This establishment of setting focuses on the outside world; although the chapter is about Frankenstein's experiment within the building, the opening line describes the conditions outside of the building before moving on to explain what happened at that time.

**Sentence 2:** *With an anxiety that almost amounted to agony, I collected the instruments of life around me, that I might infuse a spark of being into the lifeless thing that lay at my feet.*

The second sentence then moves inside the building and focuses on Frankenstein. It begins by telling us how he is feeling, then moves on to explain what he is doing.

**Sentence 3:** *It was already one in the morning; the rain pattered dismally against the panes, and my candle was nearly burnt out, when, by the glimmer of the half-extinguished light, I saw the dull yellow eye of the creature open; it breathed hard, and a convulsive motion agitated its limbs.*

Here is the overly long sentence that I analysed in question 2. Sentence three takes us back outside and describes the weather for some time before describing how the creature comes to life.

All this is fairly simple, but it is important to remember that the question is asking you to explain how Shelley uses structure **to interest the reader**. From the above summaries, we can clearly see that the topic of the writing keeps changing: it begins outside with the weather, switches to Frankenstein and then returns outside to the weather. When writers want to create tension (to make you tense and emotionally strained), they will often take their focus away from the very thing you want to know about. Shakespeare was a master at this. In many of his plays, such as 'Romeo and Juliet' and 'The Merchant of Venice', he will input small comedic scenes after huge moments of action and tension. The audience becomes more and more tense because they want to know what happens next. If a writer wants to create tension, this is just the way to do it. When we cannot read about what is happening, we begin to imagine something taking place. Each reader brings their own imagination to the text, creating ideas which (for them personally) are incredibly tense and frightening. It's the same with horror films. So, often we are most scared when we cannot see the monster because we each imagine something that really frightens us personally.

When we finally see the monster, we are often disappointed to find that it's not as scary as we had imagined.

How do we apply this to the extract from 'Frankenstein'? One theory is that Shelley structures the opening to make the reader keen to read on and to discover what happens with the creature. While the creature is clearly the topic of this extract, the author spends a large amount of time describing the setting. These moments cause the reader to become impatient and agitated, desperate to read on and to discover what exactly is happening with the creature. Let's put that idea into a paragraph:

---

**SAMPLE ANSWER 1**

Shelley uses structure to interest the reader by continually digressing from the main topic of the extract: the creature. We are introduced to the general setting of a 'dreary night of November' and, once this setting is established, the writer moves to the specifics taking place inside the building, namely the 'accomplishment of' Frankenstein's 'toils'. However, Shelley then digresses once more to the weather, explaining that 'it was already one in the morning'. This digression from the main topic is used by the writer to create tension and suspense. We are keen to read about the creature, but the author teases us by switching to another topic (and one that he has already covered) to heighten the suspense for when the creature is finally revealed later in the extract. Bereft of the facts, the reader begins to imagine the horrors that are taking place inside the building, developing the tension before what is soon to be revealed.

---

Now let's look at the second bullet point:

## HOW AND WHY THIS FOCUS CHANGES THROUGHOUT THE EXTRACT

One of the simple ways to approach this element of the question is to consider the different topics of each paragraph. The rules of writing clearly state that a writer must change paragraph when writing about a different topic, person, place or time. So in theory, each paragraph of the extract should focus on something slightly different. Let's put that to the test with our 'Frankenstein' extract:

### Paragraph 1

*It was on a dreary night of November that I beheld the accomplishment of my toils. With an anxiety that almost amounted to agony, I collected the instruments of life around me, that I might infuse a spark of being into the lifeless thing that lay at my feet. It was already one in the morning; the rain pattered dismally against the panes, and my candle was nearly burnt out, when, by the glimmer of the half-extinguished light, I saw the dull yellow eye of the creature open; it breathed hard, and a convulsive motion agitated its limbs.*

Paragraph 1 summary: this paragraph sets the scene and establishes the fact that Frankenstein is trying to bring the creature to life.

### Paragraph 2

*How can I describe my emotions at this catastrophe, or how delineate the wretch whom with such infinite pains and care I had endeavoured to form? His limbs were in proportion, and I had selected his features as beautiful. Beautiful!*

*Great God! His yellow skin scarcely covered the work of muscles and arteries beneath; his hair was of a lustrous black, and flowing; his teeth of a pearly whiteness; but these luxuriances only formed a more horrid contrast with his watery eyes, that seemed almost of the same colour as the dun-white sockets in which they were set, his shrivelled complexion and straight black lips.*

Paragraph 2 summary: this paragraph describes the creature.

## Paragraph 3

*The different accidents of life are not so changeable as the feelings of human nature. I had worked hard for nearly two years, for the sole purpose of infusing life into an inanimate body. For this I had deprived myself of rest and health. I had desired it with an ardour that far exceeded moderation; but now that I had finished, the beauty of the dream vanished, and breathless horror and disgust filled my heart. Unable to endure the aspect of the being I had created, I rushed out of the room and continued a long time traversing my bed-chamber, unable to compose my mind to sleep. At length lassitude succeeded to the tumult I had before endured, and I threw myself on the bed in my clothes, endeavouring to seek a few moments of forgetfulness. But it was in vain; I slept, indeed, but I was disturbed by the wildest dreams. I thought I saw Elizabeth, in the bloom of health, walking in the streets of Ingolstadt. Delighted and surprised, I embraced her, but as I imprinted the first kiss on her lips, they became livid with the hue of death; her features appeared to change, and I thought that I held the corpse of my dead mother in my arms; a shroud enveloped her form, and I saw the grave-worms crawling in the folds of the flannel. I started from my sleep with horror; a cold dew covered my forehead, my teeth chattered, and every limb became convulsed; when, by the dim and yellow light of the moon, as it forced its way through the window shutters, I beheld the wretch—the miserable monster whom I had created. He held up the curtain of the bed; and his eyes, if eyes they may be called, were fixed on me. His jaws opened, and he muttered some inarticulate sounds, while a grin wrinkled his cheeks. He might have spoken, but I did not hear; one hand was stretched out, seemingly to detain me, but I escaped and rushed downstairs. I took refuge in the courtyard belonging to the house which I inhabited, where I remained during the rest of the night, walking up and down in the greatest agitation, listening attentively, catching and fearing each sound as if it were to announce the approach of the demoniacal corpse to which I had so miserably given life.*

Paragraph 3 summary: this is a long paragraph that is essentially made up of a flashback to the events of the past. After the flashback, it details how Frankenstein ran away, fell asleep and dreamt of Elizabeth dying. Following this, he woke up and saw the creature again before finally running away again.

## Why is this important?

So how does the focus change throughout the piece? Most of the ideas here seem very similar to sample answer paragraph one because the topic keeps changing from the one thing we want to know about: the creature. We don't want to write the same point twice, even though it is clearly a very important point to make. So, let's move on to the flashback. Flashbacks are structural devices where a past event is fitted into the current chronology of the text. Again, there are numerous reasons for using a flashback, and here is just one of them:

---

**SAMPLE ANSWER 2**

Shelley's use of structure changes throughout the piece to create a sense of chaos and turmoil, which reflects the mind-set of Frankenstein himself. In paragraph 3, the narrator uses a flashback to revisit the past, explaining that he 'had worked hard for nearly two years' and had 'deprived' himself 'of rest and health'. This disjointed narrative structure creates a chaotic atmosphere to the piece. This is used by the author to reflect the feelings of Frankenstein, who at this point is in a state of chaos and turmoil. The structure leads the reader to feel a sense of this same chaos, as we struggle to understand what is happening and when.

---

As you can see from this paragraph, the point about structure is linked to the purpose of the writer and its effect on the reader. We refer to this paragraph structure as PEE paragraphs:

**P: Point**  Answer the question in one sentence. Be sure to use the wording of the question to show the examiner that you are clearly answering the question.

**E: Evidence**  Find a quotation from the text that proves your point. Ideally, the quotation should be short and embedded into your sentence (so that the quotations read fluently as if it they are part of your sentence).

**E: Explain**  This is the most important part of the paragraph. Explain HOW your chosen quotation proves your point.

Finally, let's look at bullet point 3:

## OTHER STRUCTURAL DEVICES

This is a chance for you to be original and perceptive. Remember, this question is asking you to assess the order of the extract, not the language. Look back at the extract and see if you can spot anything that we haven't already covered.

Here are a few thoughts of my own:

1. There is a constant reminder of the weather throughout the extract. From the 'dreary' night to the rain which 'pattered dismally', the reader is made uncomfortable by the weather, which reflects the emotions of Frankenstein.

2. The paragraphs get longer and longer as the piece goes on. Perhaps this mirrors how Frankenstein is becoming more and more overwhelmed as time goes by.

**SAMPLE ANSWER 3**

Shelley constantly reminds the reader of the weather throughout the extract. From the 'dreary' night to the rain pattering 'dismally', the reader is made uncomfortable by the continual references to weather. This encourages the reader to view things from the perspective of Frankenstein himself. By forcing us to adopt the viewpoint of Frankenstein, the reader's sense of horror is heightened when he finally beholds the creature.

Furthermore, Shelley's use of paragraph structure is used for effect. As the extract progresses, each paragraph becomes longer and longer. This reflects how Frankenstein is becoming more and more overwhelmed as time goes by. This puts an emotional strain on the reader, who struggles to keep up with the varied content of the longer paragraphs.

## BRINGING IT ALL TOGETHER

This question is asking quite a lot of you in only ten minutes. Would you be able to write all three paragraphs in that time? If you could only write two of them, which two would you use to hit the 'perceptive' element of the mark scheme? This is not an easy question to answer, as all points of structural analysis are, by their very nature, perceptive. As we will see in the guide to English literature (available at mrbruff.com), analysing structure is always a good way to hit top marks. For me, I would include paragraph 3, as it is an original point, not simply one found from following the bullet points in the question. I would follow it with the ideas in paragraph 2, and fit in paragraph 1 if I had time.

# QUESTION 4

Question 4 assesses AO4: 'Evaluate texts critically and support this with appropriate textual references'.

This question is worth 20 marks, and you should therefore spend around 20-25 minutes on it. Clearly, this is a big jump up from the number of marks available in previous questions. As a result, there will be much more to say in this answer.

Question 4 is about an extract, not the whole text. You will be given an opinion from a reader and asked to respond. You should write about your own impressions, evaluating how the writer created these impressions. Support your ideas with quotations from the text. This question requires you to write about anything that is relevant to your answer, including language, structure, tone, etc. Here is a typical question:

**Question 4**

You should base your answer on lines 14 to 37.

A student said: "The writer makes it feel as if you are inside the room with Dr Frankenstein, experiencing everything he is experiencing".

To what extent do you agree?

In your response, you could:

- Write about your impressions of Dr Frankenstein
- Analyse how the writer has created these impressions
- Back up your answers with quotations from the text          **[20 marks]**

The big concern with Question 4 is the meaning of the word 'how' in the second bullet point. The confusion lies in the fact that this is not a question assessing AO2: language and structure. So, what evidence can you use in your answer? Despite the assessment objective confusion, you can write about language, structure, tone, word choices, symbolism, sentence types, imagery and more. So, it's good news: you can write about absolutely anything that is used to inform your answer. Don't let the assessment objective put you off!

For the first time, the bullet points are not listing separate areas to focus on, but are encompassing various elements which should be covered in each paragraph. In that sense, there is less guidance with this question, so a plan of action is essential.

Look at the wording of the question. I would re-read the extract and think about this: *Do I feel as if I am there with Frankenstein? If so, why? If not, why not?*

Let's apply that to the extract and pick out key quotations:

*The different accidents of life are not so changeable as the feelings of human nature. I had ardour that far exceeded moderation; but now that I had finished, the beauty of the dream vanished, and breathless horror and disgust filled my heart. Unable to endure the aspect of the being I had created, I rushed out of the room, continued a long time traversing my bed chamber, unable to compose my mind to sleep. At length lassitude succeeded to the tumult I had before endured; and I threw myself on the bed in my clothes, endeavouring to seek a few moments of forgetfulness. But it was in vain: I slept, indeed, but I was disturbed by the wildest dreams. I thought I saw Elizabeth, in the bloom of health, walking in the streets of Ingolstadt. Delighted and surprised, I embraced her; but as I imprinted the first kiss on her lips, they became livid with the hue of death; her features appeared to change, and I thought that I held the corpse of my dead mother in my arms; a shroud enveloped her form, and I saw the grave-worms crawling in the folds of the flannel. I started from my sleep with horror; a cold dew covered my forehead, my teeth chattered, and every limb became convulsed: when, by the dim and yellow light of the moon, as it forced its way through the window shutters, I beheld the wretch -- the miserable monster whom I had created. He held up the curtain of the bed and his eyes, if eyes they may be called, were fixed on me. His jaws opened, and he muttered some inarticulate sounds, while a grin wrinkled his cheeks. He might have spoken, but I did not hear; one hand was stretched out, seemingly to detain me, but I escaped, and rushed down stairs. I took refuge in the courtyard belonging to the house which I inhabited; where I remained during the rest of the night, walking up and down in the greatest agitation, listening attentively, catching and fearing each sound as if it were to announce the approach of the demoniacal corpse to which I had so miserably given life.*

## 'EXPERIENCE EVERYTHING HE IS EXPERIENCING'

- The full sensory description of waking up creates a vivid image in the reader's mind.
- The emotive language 'wretch' and 'miserable' helps us to feel what Frankenstein is feeling.
- The overly long sentences, for example the final sentence, are confusing to the reader. This feeling of confusion echoes that of Frankenstein and helps us to feel as he feels.

As you can see, I have found points that cover language and structure. Did you spot any others? The hardest part of this question is finding the evidence from the text to back up your answer. The 'evaluate' element of the assessment objective is essentially asking you to read the entire extract and decide for yourself how effective it is. Once you've made that decision, you need to find the parts of the text which gave you that impression. Students often find this difficult.

**Practise at home:** Pick up any fiction book at home or in the library. Read the first page and ask yourself, *Is this engaging? Does it make me want to read on?* Whatever the answer, try to find evidence from the text that has made you feel that way.

If the book does grab your attention, why not read the whole thing? When a sad event happens, ask yourself if you find it sad and why. If it's a happy moment, what does the writer do to make it happy? Practising in this way will help you with question 4 of the exam.

---

**SAMPLE ANSWER**

I agree that the writer goes to great lengths to make the reader feel as if we are in the room, experiencing everything that Frankenstein is experiencing. One of the ways in which this is achieved is through Shelley's employment of a wide range of sensory description. Not only do we read what Frankenstein sees ('I beheld the wretch') but we also read about what he feels and hears. When awaking from his dream, he feels a 'cold dew' on his forehead. His 'teeth chattered' and 'every limb became convulsed'. These images relate to how he physically feels, and they allow the reader to gain a complete sense of the experience. We also read about what he can hear when the creature 'muttered some inarticulate sounds'. Through describing

---

a range of the senses—sight, sound and touch—Shelley gives the reader such a strong and detailed account of how the narrator feels that it allows us to fully understand the situation and to feel as if we are there ourselves.

Shelley also uses sentence structure to make the reader feel as if we are there with Frankenstein. The incredibly long final sentence beginning 'I took refuge in the courtyard' is made up of numerous clauses and is so long that it is difficult and breath-taking to read. This is a deliberate technique used by Shelley, who wants to convey the fact that Frankenstein is feeling overwhelmed, and this is mirrored in the sentence structure. With fifty-seven words and four commas, the chaotic sentence structure reflects Frankenstein's confused emotions. Just reading this sentence is difficult and overwhelming for the reader, resulting in us feeling very similar to Frankenstein himself.

Shelley's use of first-person narrator makes it feel as if we are there with Frankenstein. The first-person narrator allows us to know exactly what Frankenstein sees and thinks, which equips the reader with a full sense of what is taking place. When the narrator tells us how 'I was disturbed by the wildest dreams', the reader is given detail about the inner mind of Frankenstein—we would not have access to this information if it had been written in the third person.

Shelley uses paragraph length to make the reader feel as if we are there with Frankenstein. The whole extract is made up of one long paragraph, which is complex and overwhelming to read. This reflects how Frankenstein himself is feeling: overwhelmed. Just like Shelley's use of sentence length, her use of paragraph length makes the reader feel overwhelmed. As this is just how Frankenstein himself is feeling, the reader feels as if they are sharing the experience with him.

# SECTION B: CREATIVE OR DESCRIPTIVE WRITING

Section B of paper 1 contains two questions; you must answer one of the two.

You will be asked to write a creative piece that could be either descriptive or narrative. Sometimes both questions will be narrative, sometimes both will be descriptive, and sometimes there will be one of each type.

The question is marked out of 40, with 16 marks being awarded for spelling, punctuation and grammar. You are advised to spend 45 minutes on the question, with the final 5 minutes allotted for checking over your answer.

WARNING: The exam board want you to be creative and original in this question. If you are confident enough in your writing, you should not follow a formulaic approach. What follows is my advice for those of you who feel that you **need** help with this question.

## Descriptive Writing

Imagine that you are asked to write a descriptive passage based on this picture:

(24 marks for content and organisation
16 marks for technical accuracy) **[40 marks]**

There are two opening tips when it comes to descriptive writing:

1. Use figurative language
2. Use vocabulary to create tone

## 1. USE FIGURATIVE LANGUAGE

Descriptive writing is so much more impressive when it encompasses some of the figurative language covered earlier on. Let's look at two examples:

**Simile example:** *The sea was like a rollercoaster.*

In this sentence, we can see the comparative idea—that the sea is tumultuous.

**Personification example:** *The antique chair was tired.*

A chair cannot get tired, but we can see that the sentence implies it is worn out, rather than physically tired.

Imagine you are asked to describe your classroom. A basic description might look like this:

> The classroom was filled with students. Each was sitting on an expensive padded chair that looked like it would be more appropriate in an office. At the front of the room was an interactive whiteboard, connected to a computer. The students sat, eagerly watching the teacher, soaking up his wisdom.

Although grammatically correct, this is a boring piece of writing. Now let's add some figurative language:

> The room was as silent as a graveyard, save for the gentle hum of the ancient computer, which sat proudly at the front of the room. The cold chill of the metal door handle jolted up my arm like a lightning bolt.

By using a range of figurative language techniques, your writing massively improves.

## 2. USE VOCABULARY TO CREATE TONE

To improve your writing in this question, you need to create the correct tone. Often confused with mood or atmosphere, tone refers to the writer's attitude towards what they are writing about and their implied audience. If you're writing about the above picture, the tone is likely to be positive. Another picture might show a stormy seafront, and your writing might be negative in tone. There are two fairly simple ways to create the right tone in your writing:

### a. Choose appropriate vocabulary

Positive language will create a positive tone. Compare the following:

> The warm sea gently lapped against the hot sand.
>
> The boiling sea smashed against the molten sand.

Both are basically saying the same thing, but the use of 'boiling', 'smashed' and 'molten' are too aggressive and negative for such a picture. We might think of this as 'emotive language' – words used to create a positive or negative emotion.

### b. Vary sentence types

Varying sentence types can create tone. Use lots of short simple sentences to create a fast paced, tense atmosphere. Use long complex or compound-complex sentences to create a more relaxed feel. Essentially, we are using the same writing skills that we analysed in Section A of this exam. Compare:

a. It was hot. The sun shone. Birds cried.

b. Although the waves gently lapped at my feet, they were no match for the powerful sun that enveloped every atom of my being. The sand, which only that morning had been cool to the touch, had warmed into a shore side oven, baking all who lay upon it.

You'll see in the above examples that sentence length creates atmosphere. Long sentences slow you down when you read, creating a sense of calmness and relaxation. Short sentences make you speed up, creating tension and action.

OK, put all those three together: poetic language, emotive language and sentence length. Now we're ready to write a descriptive piece!

**PART OF A SAMPLE ANSWER**

Peaceful and inviting, the quiet village sits idly on the edge of the golden beach. The huts proudly bask in the nourishing warmth of the ever-shining sun. Beside them, palm trees lean towards the ocean, knowing that only its waters can satisfy their longing thirst. They stand, hypnotised by the never-ending gentle lapping of the crystal waves upon the shore. For thousands of years, it has been so.

Somewhere, a child's laughter rings in the air. It is the sound of the carefree in a village where there is no stress or strain. No internet. No phone signals. No social media. Only the ever-present gentle hum of the ocean and the promise of its plentiful bounty, caught each day by the fishermen.

Sensing that the midday heat may be too much for some, a generous tree offers sanctuary in the shade beneath its heavy boughs. The sand, dappled with the footsteps of now departed visitors, adorns the scene like a red carpet adorns a film premiere.

Now let's look at a full sample answer. This answer was written by Izzy Liddamore, who described a picture of a young queen. Izzy's use of emotive language (underlined) is particularly impressive:

She was barely twenty when the crown was <u>forced</u> upon her head, and there it sat now, <u>crammed</u> onto her pillow of cascading red curls. Those curls: curls that were once beautifully untamed, but now were so <u>ferociously glued</u> to her scalp that barely a wisp escaped the <u>iron grip</u> of her hair net. A vigorously carved parting separated her fringe, adorning her face <u>like a hideous scar</u>; it was <u>ruthlessly slashed</u> in a straight line across the top of her head. And on top of it all, a collection of <u>insipid</u> jewels that dimmed in elegance in comparison to the spiralling river of her crimson hair which spoke so strongly of her past freedom. Freedom now lost. Forever.

Concealed behind the empty pallor of her foundation lay hundreds of freckles - freckles that swirled and adorned her face like stars, stunning constellations that glowed with sheer happiness and joy. Happiness that was gone now. Clumsily, the alluring sharpness of her chin had been softened by hastily applied rouge that only emphasised her obvious fatigue, caused by the money that had transformed her into a very prosperous slave.

Her past was a distant memory.

Her face. The beautiful, uplifting melodies of her face tainted with the dissonance of royalty. For the soft and sweet hue of her cheeks had been poisoned with blood-red; the perfect cadence of her hazel eyes diminished in pools of suffering; the harmonies of her nose and lips distorted by unwanted wealth. The pearls wound so tightly around her slender neck seemed to strangle her in a discord of sheer misery. The tear-drops that hung limply from her ear lobes only served to express the cacophony of sadness that the strings of her heart played on a daily basis. Because it seemed like she would be held a prisoner on the throne she hated.

Forever.

As you can see, this answer is very impressive. Izzy's use of negative emotive language, underlined, effectively creates the impression that the young queen sees her situation in negative terms.

Look too at the varied sentence length and paragraph length. It's fantastic!

# Narrative Writing

Narrative writing means to write a story. Here is a typical question:

| Write the opening part of a story based on a tropical island. |
| --- |

It is fair to say that narrative writing should cover all the skills from descriptive writing: poetic language, emotive language and varied sentence length. However, with narrative writing it is important to be aware of the elements that create narrative.

**IMPORTANT:** If you are asked to write the opening of a story, it should not contain much action. You should be introducing the characters and setting, with perhaps one event that ties it all together. The examiner does not want to read a complete story with plot twists and action. When young children write, their stories are always filled with murder, blood, dragons, etc. Your writing needs to be subtler. You also need to avoid the most common mistake of narrative writing:

**SHOW ME: DON'T TELL ME**

Imagine you are writing a story about a drug addict. The 'tell me' style narrative would read like this:

> She was looking for drugs, desperate to get some because she was starting to experience withdrawal symptoms.

In the sentence above, I have told the reader what is happening. The art to 'showing, not telling' is to describe an event or a moment of action, making your reader infer (work out) the details, without you explicitly stating them. Now look at this:

> Her eyes searched quickly, flitting around the room; it had to be here somewhere. Her hands were starting to shake—the familiar signal from her bloodstream that time was running out. Beads of sweat rolled down her forehead, as she overturned dirty pillows and tore open empty cupboards. She reached for her purse, but she knew already what she would find inside: nothing. She screamed in desperation.

Can you see the difference? Showing, not telling, is a key part to all narrative writing. Pick up any novel or short story and you'll see it for yourself.

So, let's return to our question: 'Write the opening part of a story based on a tropical island'.

This answer can be written in many ways. What do you imagine when you read it? Perhaps a sailor is marooned on a deserted island. Maybe a luxury holiday is about to go horribly wrong. Whatever you decide, you once again need to craft emotive language and sentence length to create the right atmosphere and tone. If your story opening is going to be that of a horror story, you'll need to add appropriate emotive language to create the right tone and mood. Here are two brief examples of story openings that have a totally different tone and therefore need to be written in very different ways:

> Dark. So dark. Tom lifted his hand in front of his face but could see nothing. A fierce wind battered his aching body. Where was he? He remembered waking up in the plane just as the screaming had begun…

In this example, I have used short sentences and negative emotive language to create a tense opening. However, a 'happy' story will need to be totally different. Let's look at a full sample answer—can you pick out the emotive language?

**SAMPLE ANSWER:**

Dark. So dark. Tom lifted his hand in front of his face but could see nothing. His ears were ringing loudly. A fierce wind battered his aching body. Where was he? Although pitch black night engulfed him, the air was humid and heavy; he was not cold.

He heard a noise behind him.

Turning blindly into the darkness, he called, "Mum? Dad? Are you there?"

Nothing. Less than nothing. He was all alone. A solitary tear ran down his cheek, and it was then that he felt the unexpected sting. His chin was cut. The salty tear bore into the rawness of his flesh. Screwing his eyes shut tightly, he breathed slowly in and out. One…two…three. Half expecting it all to be a dream, he opened his eyes. No, this was real.

He remembered waking up in the plane just as the screaming began. The captain had switched the lights off for the passengers to sleep, but they had been jolted into action, waking those who were unlucky enough to open their eyes and see. Everything was wrong. The plane was upside down. A flimsy oxygen mask fell in front of his face. The plane was crashing.

Slowly, very slowly, Tom's eyes began to adjust to the darkness. He was standing on a sandy beach—unforgiving shards of coral dug into his one shoeless foot. "How did I lose a shoe?" he asked aloud, his voice echoing in the emptiness.

The ringing in his ears began to subside. Somewhere, a tap was running. No, it wasn't a tap. It was the sea.

Then he saw it: a bright yellow explosion was rising from the ocean. The sun.

As the darkness began to recede, Tom saw for the first time the full extent of his surroundings. Yes, he was standing on a beach. It looked like the front cover of a holiday brochure: white, unadulterated sand, palm trees leaning over towards the sea in a picture-perfect pose. Despite the chaos that Tom felt inside, the waves lapped gently against the shore. To the casual onlooker, everything seemed perfect. But then Tom turned around and saw for the first time deep scars inflicted on the beachfront. Flaming shards of fractured metal stuck out of the scorched patches of sand like devilish cacti in a post-apocalyptic thriller. Except this was no movie. This was real life.

Dazed, Tom walked towards what he recognised to be the tail of the plane. It looked huge—at least twenty feet tall. The edges were licked with flame, the molten metal bubbling under the intensity of the heat. "Where is everyone?" Tom whispered to himself. There had been over a hundred passengers on board that plane; where were they all? Was this some kind of joke? None of it made any sense.

In terms of writing a story opening, this answer does exactly what an exposition should do: it introduces the setting and characters. I didn't get carried away with continuing the story—very little action takes place.

I also included a flashback. The exam mark scheme dictates that students aiming to achieve the highest grades should use inventive structural features. A flashback is a simple way of achieving just that. So, in this example, the story begins on the island and includes a flashback about how the character ended up there. This keeps the reader engaged, as they want to find out whether anyone else from the plane has survived.

Now let's break down the answer:

**Varied sentence structure:** 'Dark. So dark', 'Screwing his eyes shut tightly, he breathed slowly in and out', 'Everything was wrong.'

**Figurative language** 'wind battered', 'pitch black night engulfed', 'tear ran', 'tear bore', 'unforgiving shards', 'bright yellow explosion', 'unadulterated sand', 'scars', 'like devilish cactus', 'licked with flame'.

**Emotive language:** 'fierce', 'solitary', 'rawness', 'inflicted', 'flaming shards', 'fractured', 'molten metal bubbling'.

Whether you are asked to write a narrative or descriptive piece, you should allow five minutes to check your writing for technical accuracy.

# Technical Accuracy

Around a third of the marks available for Section B in both English language examinations are awarded for spelling, punctuation and grammar. Some common mistakes and simple tips for improvement are below.

## CAPITAL LETTERS

Capital letters may seem a very easy place to start but, if you make mistakes with these apparently simple pieces of punctuation, then you will struggle to gain a high grade. There is little more off-putting and instantly recognisable to an examiner than the incorrect use of a capital letter.

You should use a capital letter for:

1. The start of a sentence e.g. *Today is the best day of my life.*

2. Names of people, brands, days of the week and months e.g. *Megan, Nike, Monday, January.*

3. Countries and cities e.g. *America, Plymouth.*

4. Languages and religions e.g. *French, Buddhist.*

5. Holidays e.g. *Christmas, Ramadan*

6. The first and significant words in a title need a capital e.g. *The Lord of the Rings.* In this example, the words 'of' and 'the' are not significant—they don't hold the meaning, so they are not capitalised.

7. The personal pronoun 'I' e.g. *Matt and I love reading.*

8. Abbreviations e.g. *BBC.*

NOTE: Some people use capital letters for emphasis e.g. *The door shut. BANG!* This is too informal and not recommended for an exam. Instead, rework the sentence. For example: *The door banged shut.*

As you can see, capital letters are not as simple as they appear to be. Why not try writing a paragraph that incorporates all eight types?

## THE APOSTROPHE OF OMISSION

This is the simplest type of apostrophe, used to show where letters or words have been taken out. Read the following example:

> I didn't even know that spiders can bite.

**Explanation:** Here, we have shortened the words *did* and *not* into the word *didn't*. In doing so, we have taken out the letter *-o*, so we put an apostrophe of omission in its place to indicate this.

The only challenge with the apostrophe of omission is that there are some words that have been shortened for so long that you might not realise it. For example: *8 o'clock* was originally shortened from *8 of the clock*. Other uses of the apostrophe make more sense when you understand how language has changed over time. For example, *shan't* used to be a double contraction *sh'n't*, short for *shall not*. Likewise, *won't* was a double contraction *wo'n't*, short for *woll not*, which was an alternative spelling for *will not*.

## THE APOSTROPHE OF POSSESSION

The apostrophe of possession shows us who or what owns something. For example:

> Your son's football is over there.

**Explanation:** because the football belongs to the son, we put an apostrophe after the word *son*.

Always ask yourself who or what the thing belongs to. Whatever the answer is, the apostrophe goes after that. For example, who does the football belong to? The answer is *son*, so the apostrophe goes after *son*.

If you can understand this simple technique, you can apply it to other examples. Where would you put the apostrophe in the following sentences?

> **The students work was awesome** (when talking about an individual student).

> **The students drama show was a real let down** (when talking about a group of students).

If you apply the technique above, it's simple:

In the first sentence who does the work belong to? The answer is the *student,* so we put the apostrophe after the word *student,* making the correct answer, *The student's work was awesome.*

In the second example, who does the drama show belong to? The answer is the *students,* so we put the apostrophe after the word *students,* making the correct answer, *The students' drama show was a real let down.*

## SENTENCE VARIETY AND COMMAS

Sentence variety is included in this section because it forms part of your SPaG mark for question 5. The correct use of commas in complex sentences links to the same mark.

The following is an absolute must for students aiming to achieve grade 9 in their English language exams. So many students fail to vary their sentence structure, and the result is pure boredom for the examiner. If you incorporate the following into your answers for Section B, your work will stand out from the rest and impress the examiner.

## 1. Beginning a sentence with two adjectives

The aim here is to start your sentence with two adjectives to describe your subject. Divide the adjectives from the rest of the sentence with a comma. For example:

Informative and entertaining, the popular book became a worldwide bestseller.

Here is another example:

Exhausted but relieved, the students finally finished their GCSE exams.

## 2. Beginning a sentence with an -ing word

Starting your sentence with an *-ing* word leads to a clause that tells us more about the subject of the sentence. Again, use a comma. For example:

Straining with the effort, Grandma did a backflip.

## 3. Beginning a sentence with an -ly word

For this third example of sentence variety, we begin the sentence with an adverb (an *-ly* word). This gives us more detail about how the verb is performed. For example:

Happily, the man whistled a tune.

Again, note the use of the **comma** to separate the clauses.

So, what would it look like if you were to use these three types of sentence in an exam response? Let's begin by looking at a piece of writing that fails to use these elements.

This is our starting text:

In a recent article, the writer argued that her make-do-and-mend generation knew something about how to save the environment. Of course, what she failed to mention was why they were making do and mending in the first place: World War 2. Oh yes, while grandma was washing her tin foil, granddad was being shipped off to Poland, destroying natural landscapes with tanks and clogging up the Polish air with fuel emissions from the machinery of war (not to mention the killing).

Here's the same text with some sentence variety added:

Disillusioned and despondent, the writer recently argued that her make-do-and-mend generation knew something about how to save the environment. Curiously, what she failed to mention was why they were making do and mending in the first place: World War 2. Hoping to be economical, grandma was washing her tin foil while granddad was being shipped off to Poland, destroying natural landscapes with tanks and clogging up the Polish air with fuel emissions from the machinery of war (not to mention the killing).

The most notable thing here is that altering the sentence structure does not alter the content of your answer–the content stays the same, but the quality of written communication is dramatically improved.

**COMMAS, CONTINUED…**

You have just read three examples of comma use in which the comma divides the main clause from the subordinate clause in complex sentences. Other types of commas include:

## 1. Listing commas

This is the one everyone knows: we use commas to break up items in a list, except for between the last two items where we use the word 'and'. The comma is correct if it can be replaced with the word 'and' or 'or'.

> The four flavours of Starburst are orange, lemon, lime and apple.

## 2. Commas for compound sentences

Commas are used before a FANBOYS (or co-ordinating) conjunction in a compound sentence:

> The boys wanted to stay up and see Santa, but they grew tired and fell asleep.

NOTE: If the sentence is very short, you don't need to use a comma:

> I love you but you're annoying.

## 3. Bracketing commas (parenthetical commas)

This is my own personal favourite use of the comma, largely because it is a simple way of making your written work seem very impressive. Use commas instead of brackets:

| Brackets | Bracketing commas |
|---|---|
| My grandmother (aged 108) lives with her daughter. | My grandmother, aged 108, lives with her daughter. |

Both sentences make sense if we take the bit out between the bracketing commas, leaving us with:

> My grandmother lives with her daughter.

Like brackets, the bracketing commas give us extra, unimportant information about the subject of the sentence—in this case, my grandmother. There is a slight difference in meaning between the two examples, however. With bracketing commas, the extra information is slightly more important.

## 4. Commas for complex sentences

When we start a complex sentence with a conjunction, we always break up the clauses with a comma:

| |
|---|
| Because I woke up at 5 a.m. this morning, I am tired. |
| If you eat too quickly, you'll have stomach cramps. |

## SEMICOLONS

Use the semicolon correctly and you are bound to impress the examiner! Surprisingly, it is very simple to use.

**1. Semicolons are used to join two sentences that are of equal importance.** A simple tip is to write a compound sentence and replace the FANBOYS (or co-ordinating) conjunction with a semicolon. This works better with 'so', 'and' and 'but'. Here are some before and after examples:

| Compound sentence | With semicolon replacement |
|---|---|
| He was tired, so he went to bed early. | He was tired; he went to bed early. |
| I checked my homework, and there were hardly any errors. | I checked my homework; there were hardly any errors. |
| She likes chocolate, but her brother prefers crisps. | She likes chocolate; her brother prefers crisps. |

**Remember:** semicolons can only be used to join two complete sentences.

2. **Semicolons introduce a conjunctive adverb that joins two sentences.** Here are some of the most common conjunctive adverbs:

| | | |
|---|---|---|
| Consequently | Meanwhile | Similarly |
| Furthermore | Moreover | Still |
| However | Otherwise | Therefore |
| Indeed | Nevertheless | |

Examples of the semicolon with conjunctive adverbs:

| |
|---|
| He ran six miles a day; consequently, his fitness levels increased. |
| I should drink more water; however, I dislike the taste. |
| She started her English homework; meanwhile, her brother learnt his times tables. |

## COLON

There are two main uses of a colon:

**1. To show that the second half of a sentence is more important than the first.** Imagine a colon as a fanfare: it announces something important.

## 2. To introduce a list, usually of subordinate clauses separated by semicolons:

> English is one of the most important subjects: it is a useful life skill, something you will use beyond school; you will access millions of words in your life time, helping you to understand the world around you and to express yourself; finally, it is, as you'll agree, fun!

So, use a semicolon and colon in your section B answers. You might want to use one of each in the first and/or last paragraph (that way, they stick in the examiner's mind).

## OTHER PUNCTUATION MARKS

While the above punctuation marks are the most commonly confused, you should aim to use a variety if you want to increase your chances of gaining a good mark. Here is a summary chart of other useful punctuation marks for Section B of both papers:

| Punctuation Mark | | Explanation |
| --- | --- | --- |
| Question mark | ? | • When might I use this? To show a question is asked.<br>• Never use multiple question marks at a time. |
| Exclamation mark | ! | • Used to show a raised voice. Example: He shouted, "Hello!"<br>• In formal English, never use multiple exclamation marks<br>• Never place an exclamation mark next to a question mark (e.g. He shouted, "Hello?!" |
| Speech marks | " _ " | • A line or two of dialogue lifts your writing in Section B.<br>• Always start a new paragraph with a new speaker. Note the use of commas and capital letters in these examples:<br>    "Where are you from?" she asked. "Why do you look so strange?"<br>    He replied, "I'm an alien."<br>• I would recommend a maximum of two lines of speech so that you can focus on crafting your ideas with interesting vocabulary. |
| Quotation marks | ' _ ' | • To quote exact words from a text. E.g. Alexander Pope said, 'To err is human, to forgive divine'. |
| Brackets | (_) | • To separate unimportant information. E.g. I bought some biscuits (chocolate) this morning. |
| Ellipsis | ... | • Ellipsis indicates a pause and slows creative writing down. For example: Surely...it couldn't be...Great Aunty Mable! |

| Hyphen | - | • A hyphen joins a compound adjective (fifty-odd teachers), a compound noun (father-in-law), and some prefixes (ex-boyfriend). |
|--------|---|---|
| Dash | — | • A dash is a common—and quite dramatic—punctuation mark. As you can see from the example, it can be used like brackets, but it emphasises the extra information.<br>• It can also be used to emphasise a point at the end of a sentence. E.g. I'm afraid I can't stay—I have to dash! |

More information about the above punctuation marks can be found in 'Mr Bruff's Guide to Grammar' at www.mrbruff.com.

# PAPER 2: WRITERS' VIEWPOINTS AND PERSPECTIVES
## SECTION A: READING

The aim of this exam is to help you understand how writers have their own viewpoints and ideas about important themes and issues.

## Overview

Section A of paper 2 focuses on reading. In this section of the exam, you will be presented with two non-fiction extracts linked by topic, but written in different centuries and taken from different genres. For example, you may have an extract from a nineteenth-century newspaper about the role of women, followed by an extract from a twenty-first-century autobiography by a prominent feminist. Source A will probably include a picture whereas Source B might be made up of two pieces.

This poses a problem, as the vast majority of students do not read non-fiction from the nineteenth century. My advice is to start now! By non-fiction we mean: journalism, articles, essays, letters, travel writing, diary entries, biography, autobiography and more.

The two sources are likely to focus on issues that have changed over time, such as: education, parenting, transport or technology.

Section A contains 4 questions: you must answer all of them. The first question is a short question worth 4 marks. Questions 2 and 3 are longer questions worth 8 and 12 marks respectively, and question 4 is an extended question worth 16 marks. As with paper 1, the idea is that the early questions warm you up for the harder ones, which follow on later.

Paper 2 of the English language exam lasts 1 hour, 45 minutes. The total mark for the paper is 80. You are advised to spend 15 minutes reading the sources, then around 1-1.5 minutes per mark available.

Let's begin by looking at our two sources.

## Source A is a newspaper article

# TEACHER IN YOUR POCKET

**An English teacher from Devon is utilising the latest technological changes to adapt to the ways students learn. Liam Murphy met the man behind mrbruff.com.**

1     I don't know about you but, when I was growing up, I learnt everything I needed to know for my exams while I was actually in school. Not that I necessarily learnt very well—the constant distraction of girls somewhat hampered my achievement. I won't tell you my exam results but, if I'd gone to an all-boys' school, I might have been a brain surgeon.

5

Andrew Bruff laughs in response, commenting: "You see, that's the problem. We take thousands of teenagers, put them in a building and expect them to shut up and listen. Not only to listen, but to concentrate, focus and learn. That certainly wasn't me at school, either." Andrew, founder of www.mrbruff.com, is an online pioneer in the world of education. He creates video tutorials for English language and literature,

10     and uploads them onto youtube.com/mrbruff where, to date, he's had over 30 million views from across 214 different countries. He must be doing something right!

"I've nothing against schools," he adds. "I love being a teacher. But the data I get online shows that students choose to study between 10 p.m. and midnight when all

15     the schools are closed. In the information age we live in, students are choosing the ways they want to learn when they want to learn. You can watch my video tutorials on your PC at home or on your iPhone on the way to school. You can download my podcast from iTunes and listen when you're walking home each day, or you can sit down to learn when most people (myself included) are going to bed."

20     Behind it all is the notion that students should be able to choose what they learn when they want to learn it. "Just because you have double English at 9 a.m. on a Monday morning, it doesn't mean you're in the right frame of mind to spend two hours learning about Shakespeare's sonnets," Andrew comments. "With my videos, students can study the entire GCSE course online. I'm not saying we should replace school, but we have to realise that students of today do things differently to any

25     other previous generation. It's not one size fits all anymore."

Having two wildly different teenagers of my own, I'm inclined to agree with the bloke. Alex, my sulky son, doesn't want to get out of bed until mid-day. Try getting a meaningful conversation out of him in the morning and you'll think you're speaking

30     to a Neanderthal. After lunch, however, it's a different story: he suddenly comes alive. On the flip side of that is Karen, my thirteen-year-old daughter, who is up and going before anyone else in the house, but flagging by 8 p.m.

And fair play to Mr Bruff, it works. Scan the testimonials page on Andrew's site www.mrbruff.com and you'll see dozens of students waxing lyrical about how his

35     videos got them an A* in their exams. When I ask him why this is, he gets passionate, practically jumping out of his seat. "I don't think the current education system is fair. It's not fair that you get an excellent education because you're in Mrs Smith's class in

room 1, but next door in room 2 with Mr Jones, no-one's learning anything. It's not fair that the quality of your education depends on your teacher, the area you live in, or whether you have rich parents who can afford expensive revision guides and
40 tutors. I want to change that, even just a little bit".

Andrew wrote and published his first revision guide in 2013, pricing it at the ridiculously low price of just 99 pence where it shot to number 1 in the Amazon best sellers chart (and has stayed in the top twenty all year long).

The father of two said: "I want to provide resources that everyone can afford, and I'm
45 doing that. I now have over twenty revision guides for sale on my site, and they are helping literally thousands of students--it's great."

When I log on to check out Andrew's videos, I'm surprised to see one of him playing Minecraft while simultaneously narrating details about the English language exam. He beams at me when I ask him about this: "Watching Minecraft videos has become
50 a national pastime with teenagers, so I wanted to bridge the gap between that and studying. Watch me play Minecraft and learn at the same time. Better still, send me your own gameplay footage for everyone to watch, and I'll narrate over that." This is a far-cry from my school days, but it's clearly working. Teenagers, teachers, schools and authors watch Andrew's videos in their thousands on a daily basis.
55
As I leave him, he has one more point to make: "This is the changing face of education. I'm just happy to be a part of it."

## Source B consists of two letters

*The first letter is from Mr Woolark, writing to the head teacher of Woodland Green School. Mr Woolark is writing to complain about his son being disciplined at school the previous week. The second letter is the head teacher's reply.*

May 9th, 1820

Dear Mr Thompson,

I was very disappointed to see that Adrian returned home today with yet more cane marks across his hands. I cannot help but feel that the school is being too severe in its distribution of discipline with a normal boy who is merely full of energy. Certainly, there are occasions when Adrian can be...distracted, but I would never
5 consider him a disobedient child.

I would appreciate you replying to my correspondence.

Yours faithfully,

Andrew Woolark

May 28th, 1820

10 Dear Mr Woolark,

I am writing with reference to the continued poor behaviour exhibited by your son, Adrian, here at Woodland Green School.

At Woodland Green, we pride ourselves on providing the very best education available to our students.

15 As you are supposedly aware, lessons begin at 7:30 a.m., with students quickly making their way to the schoolroom. It is unfortunate that Adrian seems to find it impossible to arrive at school on time although this is not why he has been reprimanded.

Each schoolroom here at Woodland Green contains as many as one hundred 20 students, who are eager and keen to learn. Students are seated at an iron-framed desk, which is bolted to the floor, facing the front of the room. Seating is tiered towards the back of the room to ensure that all pupils are able to see clearly to the front of the class. These seating arrangements ensure all students are given an excellent view of the class teacher from whom they will be learning. We pride ourselves on our teachers here, Mr Woolark, and students who do the same are 25 quick to learn, nay, to excel. Adrian does not seem to feel the same way. Twice, yes twice, he has been caught talking over the teacher Mr Butterly. Mr Butterly, himself now a little hard of hearing, was not aware of Adrian's idle chatter, but I myself was. I observed Adrian through the curtain at the rear of the room and withdrew him directly to my office to receive the cane. He was obstinate enough to inform me 30 that he knew all about the topic Mr Butterly was expounding upon and therefore had no need to listen. You can quite understand, I am sure, that I therefore proceeded to administer two lashes of 'old faithful'?

We observe the highest levels of focus here at Woodland Green. Students are 35 expected to sit in complete silence, as the teacher writes notes upon the blackboard—notes students are then required to copy. In this manner, we enrich our students with intellectual force. Most schoolroom time is allocated to the study of reading, writing and arithmetic, and there is no time for idle chatter.

Of course, we fully believe in creating a rounded child, and so once a week we 40 have drill in the playground. Most of this time is spent jogging on the spot or lifting dumbbells. Adrian should use these occasions as an outlet for his 'energy', and must remain silent in class.

I trust that this settles the matter.

Yours faithfully,

Edgar Thompson, Head teacher, Woodland Green School

As you can see, there is a thematic link between the two texts in that they both focus on education. The difference in genre is that source A is a newspaper article while source B is a pair of private, albeit formal, letters. While the topic is the same, the viewpoint is very different: in source A, the writer and interviewee believe in students taking ownership of the time and method of their learning. In source B, Edgar Thompson believes in teachers and school as the unquestionable authority in education.

Across the English language exams, papers 1 and 2, you will have a total of three sources. Between the three sources, you'll have one from the nineteenth century, one from the twentieth century and one from the twenty-first century. So, once you've seen the source in paper 1, you can work out the dates of the sources for paper 2.

## QUESTION 1

Question 1 assesses the first part of AO1: 'Identify and interpret explicit and implicit information and ideas'. This is the same objective that was assessed in question 1 of English language, paper 1 and it assesses your understanding of the obvious and subtler parts of the extract. The question is worth 4 marks, and you should spend around 5 minutes answering it. You will be directed to a certain portion of one of the sources and asked to pick out a number of truths from a list of statements. For example:

---

**Question 1**

Read source A from lines 1 to 25. Choose four statements which are TRUE.

Shade the circles in the boxes of the statements which are true.

A. Liam Murphy did not enjoy his time at school. ◯
B. Andrew Bruff makes online video tutorials. ◯
C. Liam Murphy was distracted by girls at school. ◯
D. Andrew Bruff was very able in school. ◯
E. Students don't want to learn during school hours. ◯
F. Many students access Andrew Bruff's videos after 10 p.m. ◯
G. Andrew Bruff believes schools are bad places. ◯
H. Liam Murphy makes a joke to excuse his poor exam results. ◯

---

Question 1 directs you to specific lines from which to find your answer. For example, it will say 'read lines 1-25'. You must base your answer on the section explained in the question. Remember: this is the start of the exam. With those exam nerves, it's easy to miss this crucial instruction, but you must make sure you take your answers from the correct lines. The lines will be numbered on the left-hand side of the page, and it is very easy in the stress of an exam to totally ignore this and to take your answer from somewhere else in the text. My advice is to draw around the lines to make sure you know where your answer needs to come from.

Can you pick the four truths? Some will be obvious (explicit) but some will be harder to find. These implicit facts require you to read between the lines and infer meaning—they won't be openly stated. Before you look at my answers, see if you can find the right answers yourself.

<hr/>

**Question 1**

Read source A from lines 1 to 25. Choose four statements which are TRUE.

Shade the circles in the boxes of the statements which are true.

**SAMPLE ANSWER:**

A. Liam Murphy did not enjoy his time at school. ⬭
B. Andrew Bruff makes online video tutorials. ⬤
C. Liam Murphy was distracted by girls at school. ⬤
D. Andrew Bruff was very able in school. ⬭
E. Students don't want to learn during school hours. ⬭
F. Many students access Andrew Bruff's videos after 10 p.m. at night. ⬤
G. Andrew Bruff believes schools are bad places. ⬭
H. Liam Murphy makes a joke to excuse his poor exam results. ⬤

<hr/>

Did you find the implicit answers? For example, question H, 'Liam Murphy makes a joke to excuse his poor exam results' isn't stated clearly in the text—we have to work out why he told the joke on line 4 to decide if this is true. Hopefully, you can work out most of the truths through a process of elimination, leaving out the ones that are NOT true.

# QUESTION 2

Question 2 is worth 8 marks and requires you to write a summary of the similarities, differences or views on a topic between the two texts. You should spend around 10 minutes answering this question. Question 2 assesses both bullet points of A01: 'identify the explicit and implicit meanings in a text, selecting evidence to back up your answers', and 'select and synthesise evidence from different texts'.

## SUMMARY WRITING

One of the pitfalls to avoid with this question is to make sure you don't start analysing language or the effect on the audience.

Let's look at a sample question:

**Question 2**

You need to refer to source A and source B:

Write a summary of the differences between Andrew Bruff and Edgar Thompson.

**[8 marks]**

As with paper 1, the key to hitting the top marks here is to give a perceptive answer. The key skill here is to develop inferences.

## INFERENCE

To achieve the highest marks in this question, you need to show your inference skills. Inference is all about writing something that you have worked out for yourself, not something that is stated in the text. Let's look at a sample answer:

Mr Bruff has a laugh, but Mr Thompson is serious.

While this is not incorrect, it is a very simple statement of difference. Now let's look at increasingly better answers. I will underline the examples of inference (the bits which are not explicitly stated in the text, but worked out by me).

Mr Bruff is informal, when he 'laughs' whereas Mr Thompson is more serious. The formal opening 'I am writing with reference to' shows he is serious.

Can you see what I've done here? I've inferred that Mr Bruff is informal. It doesn't tell me that anywhere in the text (not explicitly). I've worked that out from evaluating the evidence within the text. Let's take it a stage further again.

Mr Bruff has an informal attitude, as he often 'laughs' and 'beams', emphasising his passion and sense of humour. This reflects the non-controlling attitude Bruff has to education: he puts the students and their needs before himself. Thompson, however, is much more formal, seen in his formality when he is 'writing with reference to'. This formal attitude is used to emphasise the difference in status between himself and Mr Woolark to whom he writes. Thompson clearly has a defined role of authority, which he is keenly protecting and projecting in this letter.

As you can see, the above paragraph is made up almost entirely of inference: points I've worked out myself that are not explicitly stated in the text. This is the method to use if you are aiming for the highest marks in this question. Once you have your points, you simply need to frame them into PEE paragraphs.

## SAMPLE ANSWER:

Andrew Bruff believes that education should focus on the student. He criticises the 'one size fits all' approach and argues that students need to take ownership of their own learning. He believes in placing students at the centre of education and making education practices change for the changing students who 'do things differently'. This is a direct contrast to Edgar Thompson, who believes that education should revolve around the teacher. He writes 'we pride ourselves on our teachers here', suggesting that the priority in Woodland Green is the staff, not the students. This is further backed up when Adrian, a student who seems to already know the topic being taught, is given 'two lashes'. What the students know does not seem important: the emphasis is on the teachers.

Another difference between the two is that Andrew Bruff has an informal attitude whereas Edgar Thompson is formal. Throughout the interview, Andrew Bruff 'laughs' and 'beams', emphasising his passion and sense of humour. This reflects the non-controlling attitude Bruff has to education: he puts the students and their needs before himself. Thompson, however, is much more formal, seen in his formality when he is 'writing with reference to'. This formal attitude is used to emphasise the difference in status between himself and Mr Woolark to whom he writes. Thompson clearly has a defined role of authority, which he is keenly protecting and projecting in this letter.

## *QUESTION 3*

Question 3 is a language analysis question that assesses AO2: 'analyse writer's use of language, using relevant subject terminology'. The question is worth 12 marks, and you should spend around 15 minutes answering it.

By 'language', this question means words, phrases, language techniques and sentence forms. You will notice the similarity with question 2 of English language, paper 1, but be warned: this question may not have bullet points directing you to look at sentence forms. However, the mark scheme states that they **are** assessed, so include them in your answer. This question (unlike in paper 1 where you analysed fiction) focuses on the language used in a non-fiction piece. Nevertheless, your approach is almost identical. We can look at words and phrases, language features and techniques, and sentence forms. I won't cover those again here, as you need only flick back to the early part of this guide to read all about those areas. **Go back to pages 9-10 to refresh your memory.** Let's remind ourselves of some common language techniques:

### LANGUAGE TECHNIQUES

A lot of students struggle with this question, particularly with the idea of analysing 'language', which seems to be such a vague term. For those who need it, here is an acronym of language terms. **However, let it be noted that this is not the best way to analyse language.** The best way is for you to pick out any words or phrases that seem significant. If you struggle with that, you can always get ARRESTED…

### ARRESTED TO HELP YOUR ANALYTICAL SKILLS

This chart on the next page explains the acronym ARRESTED, and you should already be familiar with many of the techniques. Study it carefully.

| TECHNIQUE | DEFINITION | EXAMPLE | EFFECT ON THE READER |
|---|---|---|---|
| **A**lliteration | A group of words beginning with the same sound. | Smoking sucks | Makes the text catchy–it sticks in the reader's head. |
| **R**hetorical question | Any question in a piece of writing that does not require an answer. | Do you want to die young? | Makes the reader feel like as if the text is specifically for them. |
| **R**epetition | Writing a word or phrase more than once. | Smoking is stupid. Smoking is pointless. | Emphasises important points. |
| **E**motive language | Words that elicit a powerful emotional response. | Smoking is barbaric and torturous. | Makes the topic of the text seem overly good or bad, depending on the purpose of the text. |
| **S**tatistics | Numerical facts and data. | 8 out of 10 smokers want to quit. | Makes the text seem authoritative and accurate. |
| **T**hree (rule of) | List of three things in a sentence. | Smoking is expensive, anti-social and harmful. | Makes the text catchy–it sticks in the reader's head. |
| **E**xaggeration | Overstating a point. | One puff could kill us all. | Dramatically emphasises an important point. |
| **D**irect address | Referring to the reader directly with the pronouns 'we' or 'you'. | You need to give up smoking. | Makes the reader feel like as if the text is specifically for them. |

A much more detailed explanation of ARRESTED is in the upcoming section on question 5.

**EXAMPLE RESPONSE 1**

> The writer of the anti-smoking leaflet uses direct address in the article, asking 'do you want to die young?' The use of 'you' grabs the reader's attention and makes them feel the article is written just for them. This involves the reader and makes them want to read on.
>
> The use of emotive language persuades the reader to want to give up smoking. Words such as 'barbaric' and 'torturous' make smoking seem so bad that they are persuaded to see their habit in an extremely negative light. The writer does this to make them want to quit.

**A WORD OF CAUTION**

If you are aiming for high grades, ARRESTED should only be your starting point. With that in mind, let's look for ARRESTED techniques in source B:

**A**lliteration: reading, writing

**R**hetorical question: You can quite understand…?

**R**epetition: n/a

**E**motive language: exhibited, supposedly, eager and keen to learn, pride ourselves, excel, idle chatter,

**S**tatistics: As many as one hundred,

**T**hree (rule of): reading, writing and arithmetic

**E**xaggeration: n/a

**D**irect Address: You can quite understand...

To improve your chances of gaining a high grade, once you have spotted the ARRESTED techniques, you could also consider words and phrases, and sentence forms (see paper 1, question 2).

Before we look at a combination of all three in a sample answer, we need to understand that Thompson is trying to persuade Mr Woolark that his son deserves the punishment he has received. He is trying to influence Mr Woolark by justifying his own actions to punish the boy. He wants both to vilify Adrian and to redeem himself.

Below is a sample answer that combines analysis of ARRESTED with words and phrases, and sentence forms. I looked for single words that are used to influence; sentence forms to influence; and ARRESTED techniques to influence. Each one is then written up as PEE paragraphs.

**TOP TIP!** To create an impressive level of language analysis, consider language placement, or the juxtaposition of words. A perceptive answer not only spots the use of language, but will also consider where words are used in relation to each other.

Look back at Mr Thompson's letter, and you will see that he has used direct address with the word 'you'. This suggests familiarity between the pair. However, this is contrasted with the much more distant and formal address 'I am writing with reference to'. We could argue that this contrast is used by Thompson not only to make Woolark feel as if the head teacher cares about him personally, but also to make it very clear that Thompson is superior. Thinking about this—the placement (juxtaposition) of language to develop comparisons and contrasts—is a great way to hit top marks and to demonstrate perceptive analytical skills.

Now let's look at a sample answer. We will start with our strongest point, as we want to make a good first impression on the examiner:

---

**Question 3**

You now need to refer only to Source B, the letter by Edgar Thompson, written to Mr Woolark.

How does Edgar Thompson use language to try to influence Mr Woolark?

**[12 marks]**


Edgar Thompson uses language to try to influence Mr Woolark and make him believe that his son Adrian deserves the punishment he was given.

To begin, Thompson has deliberately juxtaposed contrasting styles of language to influence Mr Woolark. He has used direct address with the word 'you'. This suggests familiarity between the pair. However, this is contrasted with the much more distant and formal address 'I am writing with reference to'. This contrast is used by Thompson not only to make Woolark feel as if the head teacher cares about him personally, but also to make it very clear that Thompson is superior to his reader, Mr Woolark. The influence he hopes to have here is to impress upon Mr Woolark that he is acting in his best interests and should not be questioned about how he conducts his school leadership.

Secondly, Thompson uses language to manipulate Mr Woolark when he writes 'as you are supposedly aware, lessons begin at 7:30 a.m.'. The use of the adverb 'supposedly' is here used to criticise Mr Woolark as a parent, subtly suggesting that Mr Woolark may be to blame for his son's lateness. Not only does this highlight one of the wrongs committed by Adrian, but it also reprimands his father. Interestingly, Thompson's point about lateness has nothing to do with Mr Woolark's letter; we sense that Thompson is exploiting the opportunity to assert his authority from the beginning. His reference to a proven fact therefore aims to put Mr Woolark at a disadvantage from the start.

Thompson uses a range of emotive language in the letter. Firstly, there is the use of negative language to describe Adrian: 'poor behaviour exhibited' is a phrase consisting of extremely negative language. The use of the verb 'exhibited' infers that Adrian's bad behaviour is some sort of public spectacle, a performance that let down a great number of people. This negative emotive language is juxtaposed with a
---

wealth of positive terms to describe Woodland Green school. Here, Thompson employs a range of positive adjectives such as 'keen', 'eager' and 'best'. This is a highly influential use of language from Thompson, who carefully juxtaposes positive and negative language to persuade Mr Woolark that his son's behaviour is completely unacceptable in such an esteemed establishment.

Thompson uses language to sarcastically mock Mr Woolark when he refers to drill being an 'outlet for his "energy"'. The word 'energy' is placed in inverted commas for two reasons. Firstly, it is a direct quote from Mr Woolark's own letter. Secondly, and most importantly, it is placed in inverted commas to suggest that Mr Thompson does not agree that Adrian's behaviour is mere 'energy'. In this sense, Thompson is trying to influence Mr Woolark by making him question his own assertions.

Finally, Thompson uses sentence structure to influence his reader, Mr Woolark. At the end of the letter, he uses the short sentence 'I trust that this settles the matter', which sounds very abrupt. Here, Thompson employs the sentence to establish his authority and emphasise his belief that he is right. The tone of this sentence boarders on aggression and does not encourage Mr Woolark to respond.

# QUESTION 4

Question 4 is worth 16 marks, and you should spend around 20 minutes on it. It assesses AO3: 'compare writers' ideas and perspectives'. It is based on sources A and B.

NOTE: Although our example focuses on comparing different attitudes, you might be asked to compare how writers convey similar viewpoints.

---

**Question 4**

Refer to source A and source B, the letter from Edgar Thompson to Mr Woolark. Compare how the writers convey their different attitudes to education.

In your answer, you should:

- Compare the different attitudes
- Compare the methods used to show these attitudes
- Support your ideas with quotations from the text. **[16 marks]**

---

Just as we saw in question 4 of paper 1, these bullet points do not show the different areas you should focus on, but highlight the need to write in PEE paragraphs. They can be simplified in the terms **what, how and where**:

- Compare the different attitudes (**what** are the attitudes)
- Compare the methods used to show these attitudes (**how** does the writer present these attitudes)

- Support your ideas with quotations from the text (**where** is the evidence from the text?)

The big concern with question 4 is what is meant by the word 'methods'.

As we have seen, the assessment objective for this question is AO3: 'compare writers' ideas and perspectives'. The confusion lies in the fact that this is not a question assessing AO2: language, structure and form. So what evidence can you use in your answer?

It's good news: you can write about form, tone, words and phrases, irony, hyperbole, imagery, emotive language, structure, sentence structure, word class and more. In fact, you can write about absolutely anything that is used to inform your answer: don't let the assessment objective put you off! With that in mind, let's think about points to include in our answer:

**Points to consider:**

1. The relaxed, informal attitude to education of Liam Murphy, compared to the formal, severe approach of Edgar Thompson. Methods: different tone, humour and seriousness. Forms: a public article and private letters.
2. Murphy's attitude is that education is far better now than it was in his own schooldays. Thompson's attitude is that his own system of education is best. Methods: a humorous, self-deprecating tone when Murphy considers his own education versus the serious, pompous tone of Thompson.

Now read the example response on the next page.

**EXAMPLE RESPONSE**

## Question 4

Compare how the writers convey their different attitudes to education.

**[16 marks]**

Both writers value education but have different approaches to learning. Liam Murphy uses humour to express his relaxed attitude towards education. He explains that 'if I'd gone to an all-boys' school, I might have been a brain surgeon'. This use of humour shows that he sees education as something that should be relaxed and enjoyed. While Edgar Thompson also clearly values education, his use of a formal and serious tone is evidence of his serious attitude towards the topic. Even though he is writing a private letter, Thompson never slips from the formal tone, seen in such lines as 'Of course, we fully believe in creating a rounded child'.

Murphy writes in an informal tone that matches his more modern and relaxed attitude to education. He states, 'I'm inclined to agree with the bloke', which seems almost out of place, particularly considering that the form of the text is a public article. The use of language is deliberately informal, and this enforces the ideas presented in the article that we should be less restrictive with children and let them manage their own learning. Once again, Thompson's attitude is completely different. The formal tone shows that he sees education as purely a formal experience. We sense that there is no personal or informal element to his letter because he does not believe that personal feelings are appropriate in an educational sphere.

Finally, Murphy clearly believes that education today is much better than when he was at school. We see this through the use of humour and a self-deprecating tone, shown first when the writer admits 'the constant distraction of girls somewhat hampered my achievement'. This humble tone is Murphy's way of admitting that something was wrong with the education system when he was at school. It suggests that the writer believes that Andrew Bruff's methods are more appropriate. Whereas Murphy uses a self-deprecating tone, Thompson's is pompous and self-righteous. This attitude is clearly seen when he argues 'we pride ourselves on our teachers here, Mr Woolark'. The pronoun 'we' suggests that the writer feels that he and his colleagues are superior. By stating the name of his recipient at the end of the sentence, the writer gives off an air of aggression and defensiveness—a direct contrast to that employed by Murphy.

# SECTION B

## SECTION B: WRITING TO EXPLAIN, ARGUE, PERSUADE, INSTRUCT OR ADVISE

## Overview

Question 5 is the writing section of the exam. You will be asked to give your own opinion on a theme that has been raised in section A.

You will be given a specific purpose, audience and form for this question. Around a third of the marks available in Section B are awarded for spelling, punctuation and grammar, so it is not just about what you write, but how you write it.

The question will be framed as a polemic statement (a strong opinion that attacks something). You will then be asked to explain a point of view in response to this statement.

Before we look at a sample question, let's explore the acronym ARRESTED in more detail. We have already seen how useful it is for analysis with Section A of this paper. It can also help you with your writing skills for Section B of both language exam papers.

## ARRESTED to enhance your writing skills

Throughout history, writers have used ARRESTED devices for effect; you've looked at how these devices can be used to analyse texts. Now let's explore how they can be used to enhance your writing skills in Section B. Let's read some examples, as they might provide inspiration for your own writing. The following examples are taken from 'Mr Bruff's Guide to Grammar' by Kerry Lewis.

### ALLITERATION

This is where words begin with the same sound. For example:

> **S**andra the **ps**ychology teacher **s**aw **s**ix **s**wans **s**wimming.

Using alliteration emphasises points and provides the examiner with evidence that you are crafting your ideas. In this extract, the alliteration practically sends shivers down the reader's spine:

> *Resisting the slow touch of a frozen finger tracing out my spine...*
>
> —'The Signal-Man' by Charles Dickens

## RHETORICAL QUESTIONS

Why do I need to write a question that my reader won't answer? You answer it yourself. This draws attention to your point and focuses your audience.

In William Shakespeare's 'The Merchant of Venice', a Jewish man called Shylock is talking to some racist Christians. He states that Jews and Christians are the same:

> *If you prick us, do we not bleed? If you tickle us, do we not laugh? If you poison us, do we not die? And if you wrong us, shall we not revenge?*

The rhetorical questions emphasise his argument that he is a human being, just like his enemies.

## REPETITION

Writers often repeat a word at the beginning of a sentence or clause. In the following extract, 'fog' is repeated to develop a menacing atmosphere:

> *Fog everywhere. Fog up the river, where it flows among green aits and meadows; fog down the river, where it rolls defiled among the tiers of shipping and the waterside pollutions of a great (and dirty) city. Fog on the Essex marshes, fog on the Kentish heights. Fog creeping into the cabooses of collier-brigs; fog lying out on the yards and hovering in the rigging of great ships; fog drooping on the gunwales of barges and small boats. Fog in the eyes and throats of ancient Greenwich pensioners, wheezing by the firesides of their wards; fog in the stem and bowl of the afternoon pipe of the wrathful skipper, down in his close cabin; fog cruelly pinching the toes and fingers of his shivering little 'prentice boy on deck.*
>
> —'Bleak House' by Charles Dickens

A similar technique is to repeat a word and the grammar that follows. This is called parallelism. In the next example, 'no' + noun + 'so' + adjective are repeated three times to emphasise the idea of perfect love.:

> *There could have been no two hearts so open, no tastes so similar, no feelings so in unison.*
>
> —'Persuasion' by Jane Austen

## EMOTIVE LANGUAGE

This is where you deliberately choose words to make your reader feel particular emotions. With a neutral statement, we don't feel anything at all:

> A student went to school.

Let's play with emotive words and change the reader's feelings:

> A prize-winning student walked confidently and cheerfully to school.
>
> A reluctant student dragged himself wearily to school.

A sports scholar bounced energetically to school.

A lonely Year 7 student, who had no friends, limped to school, dragging his heavy bag, hoping that the bullies wouldn't catch him.

Remember that, as a wordsmith, you need to think carefully about your vocabulary and the effect that you want it to have on the examiner.

## STATISTICS AND NUMERICAL DATA

If you use statistics or numbers to support your points, this gives you authority. For example:

> *"Eight-and-twenty years," said I, "I have lived, and never a ghost have I seen as yet."*
>
> —'The Red Room' by H.G. Wells

The narrator uses the number of his age to emphasise his point: ghosts don't exist. (He sets himself up, of course, for his night in a haunted room...)

## THREE (RULE OF THREE)

The Rule of Three is the idea that things in sets of three are more memorable, more effective and more satisfying. Here are some examples:

> *I came, I saw, I conquered.*
>
> —Julius Caesar, 46 BC

> *Friends, Romans, Countrymen —*
>
> 'Julius Caesar' by Shakespeare

> *Life, Liberty and the pursuit of Happiness*
>
> —'Declaration of Independence', composed by Thomas Jefferson

If you can add alliteration to your three thoughtful thrilling words, this doubles the impact!

## EXAGGERATION (OR HYPERBOLE)

Exaggeration is used for emphasis or humour. (Hyperbole is the BEST thing!)

In this extract from Andrew Marvell's poem 'To His Coy Mistress', the narrator tries to persuade his 'coy mistress' to sleep with him. He uses hyperbole to say what he would do if he had all the time in the world:

> *An hundred years should go to praise*
> *Thine eyes and on thy forehead gaze;*
> *Two hundred to adore each breast;*
> *But thirty thousand to the rest;*
> *An age at least to every part,*
> *And the last age should show your heart;*

## DIRECT ADDRESS

Some stories are narrated in the third person. The narrator won't say **I** or **you**. Instead, the pronouns **he, she, it** and **they** are used. For example:

> *Emma Woodhouse, handsome, clever, and rich, with a comfortable home and happy disposition, seemed to unite some of the best blessings of existence; and had lived nearly twenty-one years in the world with very little to distress or vex her. She was the youngest of the two daughters of a most affectionate, indulgent father; and had, in consequence of her sister's marriage, been mistress of his house from a very early period.*
>
> —'Emma' by Jane Austen

The advantage of writing in the third person is that the author can move from place to place and narrate everything that's happening. The disadvantage is that it's difficult to get inside a character's head. Therefore, readers might not relate to the character as much.

Compare it to the following extract, which is written in the first person:

> *YOU don't know about me without you have read a book by the name of The Adventures of Tom Sawyer; but that ain't no matter. That book was made by Mr. Mark Twain, and he told the truth, mainly. There was things which he stretched, but mainly he told the truth. That is nothing. I never seen anybody but lied one time or another, without it was Aunt Polly, or the widow, or maybe Mary. Aunt Polly— Tom's Aunt Polly, she is—and Mary, and the Widow Douglas is all told about in that book, which is mostly a true book, with some stretchers, as I said before. Now the way that the book winds up is this: Tom and me found the money that the robbers hid in the cave, and it made us rich. We got six thousand dollars apiece—all gold. It was an awful sight of money when it was piled up.*
>
> —'The Adventures of Huckleberry Finn' by Mark Twain

The word 'you' (which is a direct address) in the second extract grabs the reader's attention from the very beginning. It makes him or her feel involved. The pronoun 'we' also involves the reader.

## Example of ARRESTED techniques in writing

This article argues that the elderly are to blame for today's problems. As you will see, you can use ARRESTED to make up much of your answer. Everything that is underlined is an example of ARRESTED—can you work out which bit is which technique?

---

**PENSIONERS POLLUTE!**

**As current surveys show, <u>75% of old people hold young people responsible for today's problems.</u> Gina Hobson suggests today's youth are not the key offenders; the elderly ruined the environment before they were even born.**

<u>Look around you</u>. <u>What do you see?</u> Do you, like me, see a world that is full to the brim with <u>rubbish, creating pollution by the bucket load</u>? Do you see wasteful consumerism gone crazy with an <u>insane, insatiable</u> desire to have everything? <u>Now, look up from this problem</u>; <u>who are those doing these things? Is it, as a recent survey shows, young people's fault?</u> No way.

**Make-do-and-mend**

In a recent article, it was argued that the make-do-and-mend generation knew something about how to save the environment. Of course, what the writer failed to mention was why they were making do and mending in the first place: World War 2. Oh yes, while grandma was washing her tin foil, granddad was being shipped off to Poland, <u>destroying natural landscapes with tanks, clogging up the Polish air with fuel emissions from the machinery of war (not to mention the killing)</u>.

**"Old people are to blame"**

I am a young person. I care. <u>I care about the environment, I care about pollution, I care about recycling.</u> Old people don't seem to realise that <u>80% of Greenpeace members are under 25</u>: young people care. Old people are to blame–take my granddad, for example.

<u>Roger Hobson is 81 years old.</u> He lives alone, but refuses to downsize from the three-bedroom house that he brought his family up in. This is common of many of the elderly, but you don't need a big house unless you have a family! I visit granddad once a week. I often check his green and brown bins; the recycling one is always empty.

The retired father-of-three commented: "I'm too weak to be sifting through his rubbish!"

Yet he's not too weak to get to the pub every week. In granddad's driveway is a car– <u>a big beast that guzzles</u> fuel. Like all old people, he's stubborn and refuses to walk anywhere, choosing instead to drive his <u>gas guzzler</u>. My granddad is not a rare case. He is a typical old person: selfish. His house is always <u>bathed in heat</u>, with his radiators <u>kicking out toxic waste</u> twenty-four hours a day.

<u>What's my point?</u> It isn't young people who are to blame. We are not <u>the homeowners, the car drivers, the consumers.</u> We are not those who fly around the world on holiday. <u>What do we do?</u> We go to school, we see our friends. It is the elderly who do these things–they torture and destroy the world. They <u>crucify</u> nature

in their desire for satisfaction. Yes, all young people have mobile phones, but we use them for <u>music, phone calls and the internet</u>, not like the wasteful elderly who make a call once a year.

The youth of today are the most educated people in the world; our conscience does not allow us to be wasteful.

For these long answers, you need to spend a few minutes planning before you begin writing.

Everyone plans in different ways, so I won't prescribe any set way of doing it. However, you must plan—examiners have to read them, and they can create a great first impression. If you do not plan your answer, the likelihood is your work will begin strong (with your best ideas) but get weaker and weaker as you write. A well-planned answer, on the other hand, can stay strong throughout the entire piece.

## Other considerations

### AUDIENCE

For question 5, you need to think very carefully about your audience. Consider these two very similar tasks:

*Write a letter to your head teacher in which you argue for the abolition of school uniform.*

*Write a letter for your student newsletter in which you argue for the abolition of school uniform.*

The purpose of both texts is the same: arguing for the abolition of school uniform. A good answer could be riddled with topics in this chapter. However, the difference in target audience—the head teacher or fellow students—will make both pieces very different.

The first thing to think of is the tone and level of formality you write in. You would write to the head teacher with a formal and polite tone whereas there would be room for a more relaxed tone in the student newsletter. Consider the person reading the text and how you can best communicate with them to achieve your purpose. However, bear in mind that you are in an exam—you will still have to craft your writing and steer clear of slang.

The second thing to be aware of is the art of second-guessing. This is an often-overlooked area, which basically means this:

Anticipate your reader's response and argue against that.

So, when writing to your head teacher, arguing that he or she should abolish school uniform, you would anticipate these responses:

- School uniform encourages good behaviour
- Some students couldn't afford the expense of smart clothes for school

- It's a time-honoured tradition

With this as your starting point, you then argue against these ideas. For example:

I know you will say that school uniform encourages good behaviour, but I disagree. At the moment, students are using their poor behaviour to express their individuality. Allow students to wear what they want to school, and their clothing choices will become their expression of self, resulting in better behaviour across the school.

By pre-emptively striking against your audience's response, you are effectively winning the argument before they even have a chance to make their points: it's a very clever technique, and the examiner will love it!

## SATIRE

Satire is the use of humour to attack injustice. On television, the best example is the show 'Have I Got News for You'.

Here's an example of how you can use satire in your own writing in response to the following question: *Write a letter to your fellow school students, in which you inform them of the benefits of school uniform.*

By wearing a shirt, tie and blazer, we are preparing ourselves for the world of work. Dressing up for school today shows you how to dress up for McDonalds tomorrow or, maybe for the lucky few of us, Primark.

It is a well-known fact that imposing a school uniform results in improved behaviour from students. Indeed, since introducing the blazer last year, we have been able to dispose of the behaviour system completely. One Year 7 student even told me, "Wearing a tie makes me want to be a better boy." Others have said that just slipping on school shoes stops them from swearing.

Indeed, school uniform makes us behave so well, I suggest we start wearing it at home too. The magical effect will mean we never backchat our parents again!'

Now, let's look at purpose, audience and form for Section B.

# Purpose of writing

The section B questions are based on different purposes: writing to explain, argue, persuade, instruct or advise. The purpose, audience and form in paper 2, question 5 is different to the purpose, audience and form for paper 1, question 5, in which you are asked to describe or narrate.

Here are some typical questions that you might see in Section B of the exam:

'School uniform is the number one most important factor in ensuring that students behave well and achieve academic success at school'.

Write a letter to your head teacher arguing for or against the abolition of school uniform.

> *'The youth of today are destroying this planet and its resources. At this rate, there will not be a planet for their children'.*
>
> Write an article for a broadsheet newspaper in which you explain your point of view on this topic.

## Handling polemic statements

The example questions above begin with a polemic statement, a strong opinion that attacks something. When you read the polemic statement, you are likely to react strongly to it. Consider the following:

> *'Teenagers are obsessed with social networking sites, which have a completely negative effect on their lives. Social networking sites should be banned.'*
>
> Write an article in which you agree or disagree with this statement.

When you read that statement, you are likely to have an instant reaction, either for or against. In all likelihood, you'll disagree with it. However, you shouldn't necessarily write for the side of the argument with which you personally agree. What you need to do is to think about the points you could make for both sides. You only need to think of them in your head but, for the purposes of this guide, let's write them down:

| Against social media | For social media |
|---|---|
| • Isolates users from real world interaction<br>• Can be used for bullying<br>• Encourages vanity | • Allows users to make friends<br>• Raises awareness of important issues and needs<br>• A relaxing and enjoyable activity in the comfort and safety of your own home<br>• Encourages computer literacy |

Once you've planned your ideas, it's time to decide which side of the argument to take. You should choose the side you feel you can write most passionately about. You should also choose the side you can write lots about. As the above chart shows, there is plenty to write on both sides.

## How to win every argument

The key to writing to argue or persuade is to second-guess. This means that you anticipate how your reader will respond and then argue against those points. What do I mean? Well, imagine your answer contains these three points:

1. Social media is good fun.

2. Social media keeps children off the streets.

3. Social media raises awareness of important issues/needs in society.

While there is nothing wrong with those ideas, they fail to adequately consider the audience. We can assume that the audience we are writing for is adults who don't like social media. Because of this, we need to think about WHY they don't like social

58

media–to second-guess their ideas. Think about it for a second: why do some adults dislike social media? I can think of two reasons right away:

1. Because it encourages online bullying.

2. Because it stops children from real-life interaction with friends and family/going outdoors.

So, you need to anticipate the reader's likely response, then argue against it. By pre-emptively striking against the reader's viewpoint before they can argue back, you will win the argument!

It can be difficult to argue against your reader's viewpoints, so you should plan your ideas before writing. Here are some initial thoughts:

## 1. Because it encourages online bullying

This is a very good argument, and it's not easy to counter-argue. However, we might write something about the fact that bullying takes place everywhere–not just online. We could say that social media does not make you a bully. The problem isn't social media: it's humanity!

## 2. Because it stops children from real life interaction with friends and family / going outdoors

This is an easier point to argue against. Older people constantly talk about how 'back in their day' they were climbing trees and building dens, or meeting up with friends every day to play on the street. We can argue that it is no longer safe to play on the streets, and urbanisation has reduced the woodlands and fields.

So, by second guessing our reader's response and arguing against it, we are much more likely to win an argument.

## SAMPLE ANSWER:

> 'Teenagers are obsessed with social networking sites, which have a completely negative effect on their lives. Social networking sites should be banned.'
>
> Write an article in which you agree or disagree with this statement.
>
> (24 marks for content and organisation
> 16 marks for technical accuracy)
> **[40 marks]**
>
> # SOCIAL MEDIA: BIN PLAN TO BAN!
>
> **Young people are embracing social media, as it proves a significant option for their spare time.**
>
> Recent government statistics show that a staggering 80% of teenagers now use social media sites such as Snapchat, Instagram and Twitter. Parents, teachers and politicians have voiced their concern about the negative impact these sites have on

the easily influenced, suggesting that their lives are being taken over by the obsessive nature of these sites. As a young person myself, I disagree.

To begin with, let's be clear about one thing: social media can have a negative impact. The news is regularly filled with stories of desperate teens who have committed suicide because of online bullying; however, let us be clear. Bullying, while not at all condonable, has been around since the dawn of time. Social media cannot be blamed for an age-old problem that is more indicative of the nature of mankind.

## "WASTING TIME ON SOCIAL MEDIA SITES!"

Some people of the older generation hearken back to halcyon times. Fred Jones, 82, states: "I spent my childhood climbing trees and making dens in the woods." The retired engineer (who does not own a computer) adds: "When we were courting, my wife and I went to the cinema every weekend without fail. These activities are much better than wasting time on social media sites!"

In the last thirty years, the incessant sprawl of industrialisation has reduced the green areas of the country to an all-time low, reducing opportunities for traditional childhood activities. Throwing young, innocent and vulnerable children out onto the streets to socialise is not the solution. These are streets that see abductions, violent attacks and rapes. I'm sure we all agree that any responsible parent wants to keep an eye on their children, safe indoors. Wanting a safer alternative, it's only natural that teenagers use social media out of harm's way, cocooned in the warmth of their houses.

Nowadays, is it affordable to go to the cinema every weekend? A student cinema ticket at my local cinema costs £10.60. Add popcorn to the mix at £4.60 and a small soft drink at £1.90, and I'll need a full-time job to afford the £17.10 price, just for one person. Talking about jobs, the minimum wage for under 18s is a measly £4 an hour, which means I have to work for ten hours to take my girlfriend to the cinema. That excludes the bus fares, of course—I'd need a second mortgage for that. Oh, I can't afford a first one.

## THE GREATER GOOD

Creative and original, teenagers today are embracing the richness of social media to benefit the world. Sites such as www.justgiving.com and www.gofundme.com offer a popular platform for people to give generously where there is need.

Student Molly Turner, 16, said: "Social media sites are really important. On Twitter, I read the story of the disabled man who was mugged; I contributed towards the £300,000 that was raised and retweeted the post. More recently, I learnt about politics though social media, and I understand that young people's votes made a huge difference to the snap election…I'm really looking forward to being eighteen, so I can vote!"

The issue is clear: social media is not evil.

We need to change the way we look at social media. We need to realise that young people are safer indoors, using their online skills and making the world a better place.

## ANALYSIS OF BEGINNING

The article presents ideas about the benefits of social media, and it counter-argues by breaking down the reader's objections.

Let's take a closer look at the answer again, examining the structure and organisation of ideas.

# SOCIAL MEDIA: BIN PLAN TO BAN!

**Young people are embracing social media, as it proves a significant option for their spare time.**

As a minimum, you should have a headline. To access a higher mark, your headline should contain wordplay (e.g. alliteration, puns, etc.) and you should have a strapline (the sub-heading that is under the headline). This piece is meant to be an article, so it should be structured to look like an article. This shows awareness that you can adapt your writing to the readers mentioned in the question.

In the example response, the headline summarises the view of the writer and draws the reader in with a hint of the topic but not a complete explanation. To grab the reader's attention, it contains alliteration and assonance ('bin' and 'ban') as well as internal rhyme with 'plan to ban'. The colon emphasises the second half of the headline even further. The strapline then summarises the writer's point of view in a little more detail, answering the questions who, what, where, why, how and when? Not all those points might be covered, but this strapline contains the basics:

**Young people** (who) **are embracing** (when—the present tense shows that it is now) **social media** (what)**, as it proves a significant option for their spare time** (why).

In your introductory paragraph, you need to reference the words in the polemic statement (the quotation part of the question) and then clearly state your point of view:

Recent government statistics show that a staggering 80% of teenagers now use social media sites such as Snapchat, Instagram and Twitter. Parents, teachers and politicians have voiced their concern about the negative impact these sites have on the easily influenced, suggesting that their lives are being taken over by the obsessive nature of these sites. As a young person myself, I disagree.

The statistic creates a sense of authority and accuracy. If you're trying to persuade someone, you need them to believe you know what you are talking about, and statistics help with that. There's a short sentence for effect at the end. The sentence is deliberately structured to end with the word 'disagree' so that the reader clearly understands your point of view.

## Alternative first paragraphs

Alternative ways of structuring your first paragraph include beginning with a rhetorical question, summarising the ideas in the quotation and then stating your point of view:

**Example 1**

Should social networking sites be banned? Some people believe that teenagers are obsessed with social media sites such as Snapchat, Instagram and Twitter. Parents, teachers and politicians have voiced their concern about the negative impact these sites have. As a young person myself, I disagree.

Or you could begin with a short anecdote, link it to the ideas in the quotation and then state your point of view:

**Example 2**

My 17-year-old brother's grades at school are suffering because he has been up all night on Snapchat, Instagram and Twitter. Parents, teachers and politicians have voiced their concern about the negative impact these sites have on teenagers' lives: they believe that social networking sites should be banned. As a young person myself, I disagree.

Or you could begin with the rule of three with three minor sentences or fragments. Remember to link them to the ideas in the quotation and then state your point of view:

**Example 3**

Tired. Irritable. Unsociable. My 17-year-old brother is at his worst in the morning. Why? He has been up all night on Snapchat, Instagram and Twitter. Parents, teachers and politicians have voiced their concern about the negative impact these sites have on teenagers' lives: they believe that social networking sites should be banned. As a young person myself, I disagree.

For a double whammy, I also included a rhetorical question!

**NOTE:** Some students end their introduction with a rhetorical question. Never do that. The point of an introduction is to introduce the topic and to make your point of view clear. If you end on a rhetorical question, this makes you look indecisive.

## ANALYSIS OF MIDDLE

To begin with, let's be clear about one thing: social media can have a negative impact. The news is regularly filled with stories of desperate teens who have committed suicide because of online bullying; however, let us be clear. Bullying, while not at all condonable, has been around since the dawn of time. Social media cannot be blamed for an age-old problem that is more indicative of the nature of mankind.

## "WASTING TIME ON SOCIAL MEDIA SITES!"

Some people of the older generation hearken back to halcyon times. Fred Jones, 82, states: "I spent my childhood climbing trees and making dens in the woods." The retired engineer (who does not own a computer) adds: "When we were courting, my wife and I went to the cinema every weekend without fail. These activities are much better than wasting time on social media sites!"

In the last thirty years, the incessant sprawl of industrialisation has reduced the green areas of the country to an all-time low, reducing opportunities for traditional childhood activities. Throwing young, innocent and vulnerable children out onto the streets to socialise is not the solution. These are streets that see abductions, violent attacks and rapes. I'm sure we all agree that any responsible parent wants to keep an eye on their children, safe indoors. Wanting a safer alternative, it's only natural that teenagers use social media out of harm's way, cocooned in the warmth of their houses.

Nowadays, is it affordable to go to the cinema every weekend? A student cinema ticket at my local cinema costs £10.60. Add popcorn to the mix at £4.60 and a small soft drink at £1.90, and I'll need a full-time job to afford the £17.10 price, just for one person. And talking about jobs, the minimum wage for under 18s is a measly £4 an hour, which means I have to work for ten hours to take my girlfriend to the cinema. That excludes the bus fares, of course—I'd need a second mortgage for that. Oh, I can't afford a first one.

This section second-guesses and counter-argues. The main thing to notice here is that it does not begin with the benefits of social media yet. The aim is to destroy the points of people who want to ban social media. There is a deliberate use of structure for effect through:

1. Acknowledging opposing views and destroying them with counter-arguments

2. A pull quote ("Wasting time on social media sites!") has been taken from Fred Jones's quote in the main body of the article. The pull quote acts as a sub-heading, summarising the ideas in this section. It breaks up the text, shows your awareness of the genre of writing articles, and provides an opportunity for you to show off a wider range of punctuation marks. Study the speech punctuation in articles, as it is slightly different to when you write a story.

3. The paragraph that begins 'In the last thirty years' deliberately contains a lot of emotive language to manipulate the reader and make them feel guilty. For example, 'Throwing **young, innocent and vulnerable** children out onto the streets to socialise is not the solution. These are streets that see **abductions, violent attacks and rapes**. I'm sure we all agree that any **responsible** parent wants to keep an eye on their children, safe indoors. Wanting a safer alternative, it's only natural that teenagers use social media **out of harm's way, cocooned in the warmth of their houses**'. Manipulation is a key aspect to writing to argue and/or persuade.

4. In the same paragraph, 'I'm sure we all agree that…' has been crafted to deliberately use the pronouns 'I' and 'we' to encourage the reader to agree with the point.

5. Note the use of time references, linking words and phrases to add fluency at the beginning of paragraphs (e.g. 'To begin with', 'In the last thirty years', 'Nowadays').

6. There is a sentence that begins with *-ing* to add variety (Wanting a safer alternative…').

7. Note the use of the semicolons, colons and brackets. We also have rhetorical questions and hyphens. Try not to overuse them.

8. Facts about cinema prices support the counter-argument.

9. There is humour through exaggeration and sarcasm: 'That excludes the bus fares, of course—I'd need a second mortgage for that. Oh, I can't afford a first one.

10. Short sentences and fragments are used for emphasis (e.g. 'We deserve it').

---

**THE GREATER GOOD**

Creative and original, teenagers today are embracing the richness of social media to benefit the world. Sites such as www.justgiving.com and www.gofundme.com offer a popular platform for people to give generously where there is need.

Student Molly Turner, 16, said: "Social media sites are really important. On Twitter, I read the story of the disabled man who was mugged; I contributed towards the £300,000 that was raised and retweeted the post. More recently, I learnt about politics though social media, and I understand that young people's votes made a huge difference to the snap election…I'm really looking forward to being eighteen, so I can vote!"

The issue is clear: social media is not evil.

---

Having presented my counter-arguments, the next part is structured to explain the good sides to social media:

1. There is now a subheading to introduce the main ideas in this section. Note the use of alliteration ('greater good') and how the adjective 'good' contrasts with 'evil' further down.

2. There's more alliteration with 'popular platform' to emphasise the point.

3. Sentence structure is varied by starting with two adjectives ('Creative and original').

4. There are bracketing commas with Molly's age.

5. There is variety of punctuation with speech marks, ellipsis and the colon.

6. There is a very short paragraph of one line to emphasise a point.

**ANALYSIS OF END**

> We need to change the way we look at social media. We need to realise that young people are safer indoors, using their online skills and making the world a better place.

This last paragraph concludes the writing, but isn't so blunt as to begin with: 'To conclude, I would say that...'.

# Form: article

We've looked at the features of an example article. Now let's remind ourselves of what you need to include with other forms.

If you are asked to write an article of any kind (newspaper, magazine, webpage, etc.), you should use the following features:

Your strapline should summarise the whole article in one or two sentences. At the very least, we want to know who, what, when, and why.

Your headline should be short, snappy and alliterative. It should hint at your point of view about the topic of the story but not give too much away.

Your introductory paragraph references the quotation in the question and firmly states your point of view.

**PENSIONERS POLLUTE!**

**As current surveys show, 75% of old people hold young people responsible for today's problems. Gina Hobson suggests today's youth are not the key offenders; the elderly ruined the environment before they were even born.**

Look around you. What do you see? Do you, like me, see a world that is full to the brim with rubbish, creating pollution by the bucket load? Do you see wasteful consumerism gone crazy with an insane, insatiable desire to have everything? Now, look up from this problem; who are those doing these things? Is it, as a recent survey shows, young people's fault? No way.

A sub-heading to summarise the next section

**Make-do-and-mend**

In a recent article, it was argued that the make-do-and-mend generation knew something about how to save the environment. Of course, what the writer failed to mention was why they were making do and mending in the first place: World War 2. Oh yes, while grandma was washing her tin foil, granddad was being shipped off to Poland, destroying natural landscapes with tanks, clogging up the Polish air with fuel emissions from the machinery of war (not to mention the killing)

A sub-heading in the form of a pull-quote. It summarises the next section

**"Old people are to blame"**

I am a young person. I care. I care about the environment, I care about pollution, I care about recycling. Old people don't seem to realise that 80% of Greenpeace members are under 25: young people care. Old people are to blame–take my granddad, for example.

The rest of your article should provide more detail about the topic. Ideally, it should include between one and two quotations from interviews with relevant people (you make these up).

# Form: Letter

Now that we have looked at how to write an article, we're going to review the other forms that you might be asked to use in the exam. Let's start with a letter.

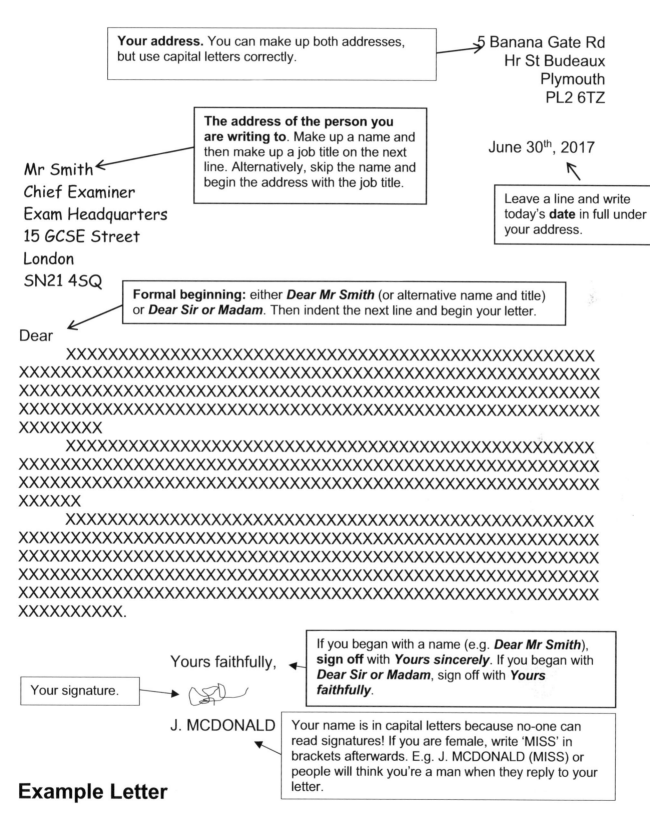

**Your address.** You can make up both addresses, but use capital letters correctly.

5 Banana Gate Rd
Hr St Budeaux
Plymouth
PL2 6TZ

June 30th, 2017

Leave a line and write today's **date** in full under your address.

**The address of the person you are writing to**. Make up a name and then make up a job title on the next line. Alternatively, skip the name and begin the address with the job title.

Mr Smith
Chief Examiner
Exam Headquarters
15 GCSE Street
London
SN21 4SQ

**Formal beginning:** either *Dear Mr Smith* (or alternative name and title) or *Dear Sir or Madam*. Then indent the next line and begin your letter.

Dear

XXXXXXXXXXXXXXXXXXXXXXXXXXXXXXXXXXXXXXXXXXXXXXXXXXXXX
XXXXXXXXXXXXXXXXXXXXXXXXXXXXXXXXXXXXXXXXXXXXXXXXXXXXX
XXXXXXXXXXXXXXXXXXXXXXXXXXXXXXXXXXXXXXXXXXXXXXXXXXXXX
XXXXXXXXXXXXXXXXXXXXXXXXXXXXXXXXXXXXXXXXXXXXXXXXXXXXX
XXXXXXX
XXXXXXXXXXXXXXXXXXXXXXXXXXXXXXXXXXXXXXXXXXXXXXXXXXXXX
XXXXXXXXXXXXXXXXXXXXXXXXXXXXXXXXXXXXXXXXXXXXXXXXXXXXX
XXXXXXXXXXXXXXXXXXXXXXXXXXXXXXXXXXXXXXXXXXXXXXXXXXXXX
XXXXX
XXXXXXXXXXXXXXXXXXXXXXXXXXXXXXXXXXXXXXXXXXXXXXXXXXXXX
XXXXXXXXXXXXXXXXXXXXXXXXXXXXXXXXXXXXXXXXXXXXXXXXXXXXX
XXXXXXXXXXXXXXXXXXXXXXXXXXXXXXXXXXXXXXXXXXXXXXXXXXXXX
XXXXXXXXXXXXXXXXXXXXXXXXXXXXXXXXXXXXXXXXXXXXXXXXXXXXX
XXXXXXXXXXXXXXXXXXXXXXXXXXXXXXXXXXXXXXXXXXXXXXXXXXXXX
XXXXXXXXX.

If you began with a name (e.g. *Dear Mr Smith*), **sign off** with *Yours sincerely*. If you began with *Dear Sir or Madam*, sign off with *Yours faithfully*.

Yours faithfully,

Your signature.

J. MCDONALD

Your name is in capital letters because no-one can read signatures! If you are female, write 'MISS' in brackets afterwards. E.g. J. MCDONALD (MISS) or people will think you're a man when they reply to your letter.

# Example Letter

Imagine this is the question for question 5:

> 'School uniform is the number one most important factor in ensuring that students behave well and achieve academic success at school'.
>
> Write a letter to your head teacher, arguing for or against the abolition of school uniform.
>
> (24 marks for content and organisation
>
> 16 marks for technical accuracy)
>
> **[40 marks]**

This is typical of the kind of question you will get in the exam; it is something everyone can answer. The exam board has to set general questions that everyone is guaranteed to understand, so be prepared for that.

You should begin with a plan of your ideas; you can do this in bullet points if you like. Spend about five minutes thinking about the question and coming up with four or five points you are going to make, along with a reminder of the skills you are going to use (e.g. ARRESTED) and the range of punctuation marks and sentence types that you are going to include.

My plan would look something like this:

- Uncomfortable—itchy jumpers, choking tie
- Expensive—many families can't afford uniform
- America—no uniform, and they are very successful

- ARRESTED, : ; — ... "—", ? ! () varied sentences, short paragraph for emphasis, linking words/phrases, wide vocabulary

---

**A 'GOOD' SAMPLE ANSWER:**

Dear Mr Smith,

I am writing to you to argue that we should be able to wear what we want to school. Do you like being uncomfortable? Well, I feel uncomfortable every single day. The school jumper is torture! It's so itchy that I come out in a rash whenever I put it on. The only person I know who wears itchy woollen jumpers like that is my granddad, so why are you making me wear one? The tie is also very uncomfortable—I feel half choked most of the time. Wearing a tie is a health and safety hazard, especially considering that there are 1,400 of us moving around the building every hour. The chances of us getting caught on something and choked (not to mention those mean bullies doing the same) is worryingly high.

In a recent survey, 85% of students in the UK said they would like to wear their own clothes to school. You cannot ignore this! I know you will probably think that students who wear their own clothes will misbehave in school, but I disagree. I think that students will behave more maturely if you treat them more maturely by letting them

---

make their own choices over what they wear. You may not think it, but students are mature, intelligent and responsible.

America is the most powerful country in the world, the market leader in industry and guess what? Students in America wear their own clothes to school. Surely this is a clear sign that what children wear to school has no influence on how they go on to perform in future life.

Finally, did you know that 65% of students in our school come from a one-parent family? How are these parents supposed to afford school uniform? By the time you buy the PE kit, parents can spend as much as £200 on uniform. If you let students wear their own clothes, then they wouldn't have any extra costs—they already have these clothes at home, so it won't be adding to their shopping expenses.

I hope you will agree with my thoughts.

Yours sincerely,

Erin Taylor

---

So, what makes this a successful answer? Well, there are at least four things it does very well:

1. Follows some of the letter form.

2. Uses ARRESTED–each paragraph is based on ARRESTED.

3. Is broken into paragraphs, with each paragraph focusing on a different part of the argument.

4. Uses some variety of punctuation.

However, the writer has not really consulted the plan in much detail, there are too many rhetorical questions, and the addresses and date are missing. The above example was good, but the example on the next page is better.

22 Oakwood Lane
Burntwood
Surrey
RH2 8PQ

11th July, 2017

Mr Smith
Head teacher
Vunderschool School
27, Pine Road
Burntwood
Surrey
RH2 9AG

Dear Mr Smith,

Responsible and mature, the young adults at Vunderschool are eagerly looking for ways to prove to you just how trustworthy we are. Will you give us the chance? Clearly, this is a great opportunity for you to strengthen your relationship with the student body. Because you are undoubtedly a busy man, I will get straight to the point: I am writing to ask you to consider the abolishment of school uniform.

In a recent Vunderschool survey, 85% of students said they want to wear their own clothes to school; this statistic cannot be ignored. As I walked past your office this morning, I was reminded of our school motto: 'Developing independence is the route to success'. Well, what better way to create independence in students than by letting us choose our own clothes?

Yesterday, a teacher asked me, "What exactly is wrong with the school uniform?" Well, I'm glad he asked. To begin with, the jumper is so itchy I would not be surprised to learn that it is made from loft insulation material. The tie is a health and safety hazard—it threatens to choke us on an hourly basis. There are 1,400 students at Vunderschool who travel around the building every hour; I think this is an accident waiting to happen. And the trousers are just ridiculous. (Rigid and cold, I feel like I am wearing a pop-up tent rather than a pair of trousers).

I imagine you will say that school uniform encourages good behaviour, but I disagree. At the moment, students are using their poor behaviour to express their individuality. Allow students to wear what they want to school, and their clothing choices will become their expression of self, resulting in better behaviour across the school. Have you ever been into the city centre and seen the youths who frequent the sundial? These teens wear long leather jackets and black boots. On first inspection, they may seem intimidating, but nothing could be further from the truth; these children do not engage in antisocial behaviour! They simply spend time together with their friends.

You see, their clothes are expressing their individuality.

Can I ask about your career aspirations for your students? I imagine you want us to be rich and successful. Well I have bad news—by making us all wear the same uniform day in, day out, you are simply preparing us for workplaces that do the same, namely fast food restaurants and shops. You see, the high-powered business people and entrepreneurs of this world choose their own clothes. Indeed, you have the freedom to choose your own suits, your own shirts, your own ties (even the

70

whacky ones you wear every Friday). You are operating within the constraints of a dress-code, but you wear what you choose. We deserve the same. Give us a dress code, but don't keep us in this barbaric uniform.

You may also feel that wearing our own clothes would lead to a reduction in our academic achievement. To prove you wrong, I need only point to our transatlantic cousins in America. America is the richest, most powerful and most successful nation in the world, and guess what: school students wear what they want to school. Surely this proves that there is no link between what we wear to school and how we will succeed in life.

Thank you for considering my letter; I look forward to your reply.

Yours sincerely

ERIN TAYLOR (MISS)

OK, so how did this answer achieve more than the previous one? It comes down to five points:

1. Form: this uses all the features of a formal letter.

2. Second guessing: throughout the letter, the writer anticipates how the headmaster will respond and pre-emptively argues against those points.

3. Sentence variety: the two adjective openings and adverb openings are used occasionally, as is a short sentence for effect. This careful crafting of sentences will set your work apart from the rest.

4. There is a paragraph of just one sentence for impact.

5. Punctuation: there is a wider range of punctuation.

6. Complex points: the points made are a little more sophisticated than in the previous example. To access the full range of marks, you need to spend a little longer planning to ensure you have sophisticated ideas that you can use.

# Form: speech

In Section B, you might be asked to write a speech for a radio programme, a hall full of people, or another situation that is stated in the question.

Your speech needs to show that you are aware that you are addressing your listeners. To do this, reference your listeners throughout. Here are some ideas, but I am sure you can add many of your own to the list:

## BEGINNING YOUR SPEECH

- Good morning, ladies and gentlemen. Thank you for coming.
- Hello, everyone. Thank you for joining me on this bitterly cold afternoon.
- Hello, listeners! This is Jo Bloggs on Radio MRB. Today, I'm going to talk about…

## MIDDLE

- I can see that the lady with the hat is shaking her head. Please bear with me—I'm coming to that point now.
- What do I mean by this? Well,…
- You might be wondering…
- I am sure that many listeners will agree that…

You should also weave in other rhetorical devices such as those in ARRESTED to show an awareness that you are crafting your ideas for your audience.

## ENDING YOUR SPEECH

- Thank you for listening.
- Thank you for listening. Does anyone have any questions?
- Thank you for listening to Radio MRB. If you have any questions, please phone, text or email—I'd love to hear from you!
- 

## SEQUENCING YOUR IDEAS

Just a reminder that your ideas should be in a logical sequence and contain linking words and phrases to add fluency (Firstly, Furthermore, Moreover, However, In contrast, To conclude, etc.).

### Example Speech
Let's look at another sample question:

> *'Technology has no place in education. Students should not take their phones to school under any circumstances'.*
>
> Write a speech for your local radio station in which you persuade your listeners that you agree **or** disagree with this view.
>
> (24 marks for content and organisation
> 16 marks for technical accuracy)
> **[40 marks]**

Once again, you should start with a plan. In your plan, you should aim to come up with four or five good points, along with a reminder of the skills you will want to use. Some example points:

- Use the calculator feature for maths
- Use the camera to take photos of homework (a 'virtual planner')
- Use reminders for homework deadlines
- Go online for research purposes
- Access existing online revision materials

---

**A 'GOOD' SAMPLE ANSWER:**

Hello, listeners. 90% of students in the UK own a mobile phone, but only 60% of them take them to school every day. I believe that mobile phones can really help children to achieve their potential, and I will tell you why.

Firstly, mobile phones can be of great use in a Maths lesson. Nearly every lesson I have in Maths requires me to use a calculator. Do you know how much a graphic calculator costs? No, neither do I. I don't need to know. I have my own calculator built into my phone. Not only does this save money from buying a calculator separately, but it also saves me valuable space in my bag. There is one boy in class who has a graphic calculator and it is huge! What's the point? He needs a phone.

Another great use of mobile phones in school centres around the camera. If you don't have your homework planner, you can simply take a photo of your homework off the board. Cameras on phones can also be used to record so, with the teacher's permission, we can now record parts of lessons where we know the teacher is saying something really important.

I only got my phone last year. Before that, I was always late handing in my homework but not anymore! Do you know why? Because I use the reminders and alarms on my phone to remind me when to do the work. Wouldn't you like it if children never got into trouble again for late work? Well the answer is simple: buy them a phone.

The final reason all students should have a phone and take it to school is because they promote safety. If there is ever a problem, or if students have or witness an accident on the way to or from school, then they can use their phone.

So, I hope you can see that phones really are the way forward, and I hope you will let your child take one to school. Thank you for listening.

OK, that was a very simple answer:

1. It has directly addressed the listeners at the beginning and end.
2. It has used some rhetorical questions to engage the listeners.
3. It has used ARRESTED.
4. It has made a range of different points, which are clearly expressed.

Unfortunately, there is much it didn't do.

Now read the following answer, which is worth more marks. Try and pick out the differences, thinking carefully about what makes this next piece better.

---

**A BETTER SAMPLE ANSWER:**

Good morning, listeners. Thanks for tuning in to Radio MRB to listen to the controversial subject of… the role of technology in education!

If you remember blackboards and chalk, you may be surprised to hear that today's schools have undergone many changes. Gone are the blackboards and OHPs; in are the iPads and interactive whiteboards. Yes, the schools of today are unrecognisable from their historic counterparts. (In fact, walking through a twenty-first-century school feels more like walking through a fancy Apple Store in a shopping centre.) Modern and exciting, the technological age is upon us. More than ever before, students are utilising technology to own their learning; there are exciting opportunities for your children to use technology in education.

If you're a parent or grandparent, the best interests of the younger members of your family will be at heart. Some of you will be comfortable with new technology but other listeners might feel intimidated and overwhelmed. Well, let me help you with that. Students today need to do many things: these can all be achieved with a simple, off-the-shelf mobile phone. If you buy your child a smartphone, it really will smarten up your child.

Firstly, I wonder how many of you got into trouble at school because you forgot to take your calculator (or—dare I ask—slide rule?) to maths. Imagine your child is sitting in a maths class and has the same experience. No calculator? Problem solved! Calculators are built into mobile phones. Now, imagine it's homework time. The homework is written on the board for your lovely son or daughter to copy up…whoops! Where's that homework planner? Is it the same one that was soaked in the bottom of their school bag when that water bottle leaked? Well, it doesn't matter: they can use their phone to take a photo of it.

But it doesn't stop there: studies show that students who have access to technology learn at a faster rate.

Although it gets a bad press, the internet is a wonderful place these days. Sites such as mrbruff.com are packed with revision videos, ebooks and podcasts, which help thousands of students to achieve their exam potential. Don't you want the same for your child? All they need is a phone—they can even access the school wi-fi for free, meaning they're not racking up a high bill. With school safety filters in place, there is no chance of them finding something inappropriate online.

Think back to your own education—wouldn't you have loved the chance to use the internet, take photos, set reminders and more? Well, you can make that dream become a reality for your child.

A caller has just rung in to share her story. Mrs Spencer from London says 'My 11-year-old daughter has a mobile phone for safety reasons: she can ring me if there's a problem. I can also get in touch with her if I need to!'. This is an important point,

---

74

and I know you want your child to be safe. The average contract price of £15 a month is nothing compared to the peace of mind you will receive, knowing that your child can contact you whenever they need to.

In conclusion, not only is a mobile phone useful for security reasons, but it's also incredibly useful for school. Thank you for listening, and we look forward to hearing more of your thoughts after the commercial break. Remember: a smart parent buys a smartphone for a techno-smart child!

This is a better answer because it pays attention to its audience, the listeners, and second-guesses their likely responses. The vocabulary and tone are also very persuasive, with emotive language deliberately used to manipulate the listeners' response. On top of that, there is a more sophisticated range of punctuation and sentence variety as well as a paragraph of one sentence for emphasis. In your Section B response, you should aim to go beyond the basics of ARRESTED and write the most sophisticated answer you can.

# Form: Essay

I am sure that you are well used to writing essays at school by now. A reminder that you should include:

**An introduction:** choose from the range of introductions illustrated earlier in this section in the 'Social Media: Bin Plan to Ban!' article. To summarise, they were:

- Start with facts or statistics
- Start with a rhetorical question
- Start with an anecdote
- Start with three minor sentences

Whichever you choose, you still need to reference the polemic statement (the quotation in the question) and then state your point of view. A punchy introduction grabs the interest of your reader.

**Middle:** your ideas should be well organised and show a logical sequence of thought. Remember to use linking words and phrases!

**End:** At the end, do not repeat everything that you have just written. Summarise your thoughts, referencing the key words of the question, in a sentence or two.

## Example Essay

Let's look at another sample question:

'We should support the British economy by only taking holidays in the UK.'

Write an essay, explaining why you agree or disagree with the statement.

**NOTES**

1. Because the question asks you to **explain**, your tone is more muted and academic: you are not persuading your reader to change their mind. You are simply asked to state your views.
2. You need to recognise and dismiss opposing arguments, as this shows more sophisticated, higher-level thinking.
3. Note that this is not a comparative essay (discussing the pros and cons). Just argue your point of view, acknowledging and dismissing the views of others as a starting point.


**EXAMPLE RESPONSE**

Rain. Coldness. Boredom. These words spring to mind when I think of a holiday in the UK. What's the point of planning a summer holiday by the beach when we can't guarantee the weather? Clearly, the British tourism industry would benefit from my money, but there's nothing worse than a British seaside in the rain. I believe that we should not be pressured to take holidays just within the UK: we should make the most of opportunities to take holidays abroad.

There are some people who only take holidays in the UK. My 78-year-old grandmother, for example, has never been abroad in her life. She says, 'What's the point in going abroad when there are so many places to visit in country?' This is a valid point—I can't claim to have visited the Orkney Islands and the Outer Hebrides. I will do, one day.

They're on my list, but there are just so many other places I want to visit first.

I want to ride a camel to the pyramid of Giza; trek in the amazing Amazon jungle; bask in the blazing sun of a beach in the Bahamas. Yes, there's a lot we can do in the UK. But there's also a lot we can do elsewhere.

I need to stress that I'm not unpatriotic. On a gloriously sunny day, I love the natural beauty of the Lake District, the craggy mountains of Scotland and Wales, and the busy historic cities and towns that form the rich tapestry of our cultural heritage. I just don't like rain. It's a well-known fact that, on average, there are 107 days of rainfall in the UK a year. 107 days! That's nearly one day in every three! That's a third of my life! I spend so much of my time shivering in school or huddled against the gas fire at home in our tiny flat that I dream of being somewhere sunny. Surely, I have the right to look forward to a holiday in a hot country?

Furthermore, we all know that after Brexit the UK will become more isolated from mainland Europe. Travelling with unrestricted movement across Europe, now is the time to make the most of opportunities while they last. I believe that we can learn a lot about other people and cultures through travel: I believe that travel broadens the mind. (I was hoping to cut costs and do my degree in a European university; unfortunately, that won't be happening anymore.)

So, excited and passionate about foreign travel, I shall close my ears to those who think I should stay in the UK. I intend to go backpacking around Europe this summer.

I'm going to practise my French and German, which I am hoping to study at university and, most of all, I'm going to enjoy the sun.

## Form: Leaflet

If you're asked to write a leaflet, you will only be expected to write the text. Don't waste time drawing columns or pictures because you won't receive any marks for this. To access the higher marks, your writing should contain the following features:

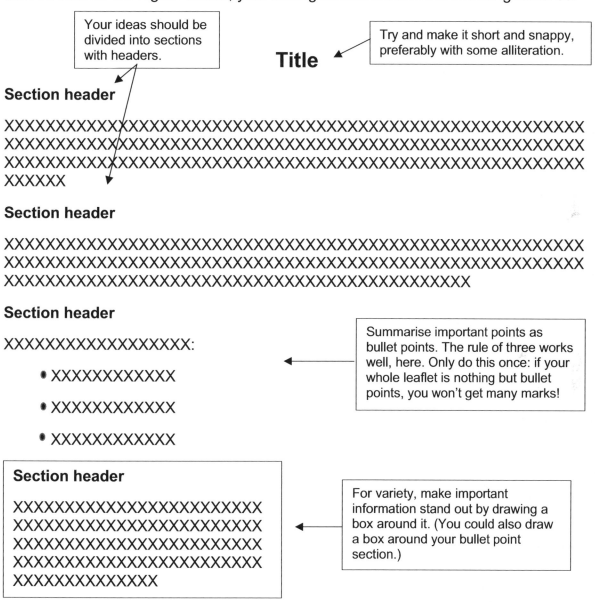

Your ideas should be divided into sections with headers.

**Title**

Try and make it short and snappy, preferably with some alliteration.

**Section header**

XXXXXXXXXXXXXXXXXXXXXXXXXXXXXXXXXXXXXXXXXXXXXXXXXXX
XXXXXXXXXXXXXXXXXXXXXXXXXXXXXXXXXXXXXXXXXXXXXXXXXX
XXXXXXXXXXXXXXXXXXXXXXXXXXXXXXXXXXXXXXXXXXXXXXXXXX
XXXXXX

**Section header**

XXXXXXXXXXXXXXXXXXXXXXXXXXXXXXXXXXXXXXXXXXXXXXXXXX
XXXXXXXXXXXXXXXXXXXXXXXXXXXXXXXXXXXXXXXXXXXXXXXXXX
XXXXXXXXXXXXXXXXXXXXXXXXXXXXXXXXXXXXXX

**Section header**

XXXXXXXXXXXXXXXXXX:

- XXXXXXXXXXX
- XXXXXXXXXXX
- XXXXXXXXXXX

Summarise important points as bullet points. The rule of three works well, here. Only do this once: if your whole leaflet is nothing but bullet points, you won't get many marks!

**Section header**

XXXXXXXXXXXXXXXXXXXXXXXXXX
XXXXXXXXXXXXXXXXXXXXXXXXXX
XXXXXXXXXXXXXXXXXXXXXXXXXX
XXXXXXXXXXXXXXXXXXXXXXXXXX
XXXXXXXXXXXXXX

For variety, make important information stand out by drawing a box around it. (You could also draw a box around your bullet point section.)

**Section header**

XXXXXXXXXXXXXXXXXXXXXXXXXXXXXXXXXXXXXXXXXXXXXXXXXXXXXX
XXXXXXXXXXXXXXXXXXXXXXXXXXXXXXXXXXXXX

The purpose of leaflets is to persuade, inform or advise. To familiarise yourself with the layout and writing style of leaflets, collect and study some!

## Example Leaflet

Here's another sample question:

---

*'We should support the British tourism industry by promoting holidays in the UK.'*

Write a leaflet, advising tourists about the best places to visit in your local area and/or surroundings.

(24 marks for content and organisation

16 marks for technical accuracy)
**[40 marks]**

---

# Lost in London? Read our Travel Tips!

## London

Samuel Johnson, an eighteenth-century English writer, once said, 'When a man is tired of London, he is tired of life'. There's something for everyone in London. It's an exciting metropolis, teeming with entertainment, full of history and offering many sightseeing opportunities. Lost and confused, some visitors are so overwhelmed that they don't know where to begin. Here is some useful advice for a hassle-free holiday.

## Getting around

Tired, weary and footsore, some tourists underestimate the size of the 25th largest city in the world. Why not make things easy for yourself with a hop-on, hop-off bus tour? This is the most economical way to learn about London, and it's a great way to gain your bearings and to sight-see at the same time! If you stop at St. Paul's Cathedral and you fancy going inside, for example, simply hop off, visit the cathedral and then hop on the next bus!

---

**Example landmarks on the hop-on, hop-off bus tour:**
- The Tower of London
- Buckingham Palace
- Big Ben (near the Houses of Parliament)

---

## Travel on a Shoestring

Travelling on a budget? There are many free attractions in London, some of which are the best art galleries and museums in the world. Browse the collections at the Tate Modern, the British Museum, the Science Museum and the Natural History Museum—these are very popular with children.

## Eating

Since the Romans founded London in AD 43, the city has grown from a tiny settlement to a population of over 8 million people. A vibrant multicultural community,

Londoners offer a wide range of food to suit your taste. Try authentic Chinese food in Chinatown or a mouth-watering curry in Little India. Alternatively, if you'd like to soak up the atmosphere of waterside cafes and pubs, why not stroll along the pretty streets and relaxing canal area of Little Venice?

There's something for everyone in London!

---

**We hope that you find this leaflet useful; for more information, contact:**

Laughing in London Tourism Board
9, Covent Garden
London
W1

www.LILTB.co.uk
info@LILTB.co.uk
Tel: 020 222 222

**We're happy to help!**

---

# Final comment about Section B

**IMPORTANT!**

With both exam papers, Section B is marked with the same mark scheme. This means that no matter which form you use in your writing, you still need to craft your ideas, using interesting vocabulary, ARRESTED and other rhetorical devices, figurative language, linking words and phrases, varied punctuation, varied sentence types, etc.

**Around a third of the marks for Section B are for SPaG, so you should allow time to check the accuracy of your writing.**

If you need to brush up on your grammar, you might want to buy 'Mr Bruff's Guide to Grammar' which is available on www.mrbruff.com as an ebook, or on Amazon as an ebook or paperback.

**Sample paper 1:**

> This extract is from the beginning of a short story by John Trevena. It is the early 1900s and Brightly, a homeless dealer in rabbit skins, is walking through the countryside.

1  Up the road from Brentor to St. Mary Tavy came Brightly, his basket dragging on his arm. He was very tired, but there was nothing unusual in that. He was tired to the point of exhaustion every day. He was very hungry, but he was used to that too. He was thinking of bread and cheese and cider; new bread and soft cheese, and cider with a rough edge to it. He licked his lips, and tried to believe he was tasting them. Then he began to cough. It was a long, heaving cough, something like that of a Dartmoor pony. He had to put his basket down and lean over it, and tap at his thin chest with a long raw hand.

8  Brightly had a home. The river saw to that; not the Tavy, but the less romantic Taw. On the Western side of Cawsand are many gorges* in the great clefts* cut by the Taw between Belstone and Sticklepath. There narrow and deep clefts have been made by the persistent water draining down to the Taw from the bogs above. In the largest of these clefts Brightly was at home. The sides were completely hidden by willow-scrub, immense ferns, and clumps of whortleberries, as well as by overhanging masses of granite. The water could be heard dripping below like a chime of fairy bells. In winter the cleft appeared a white cascade of falling water, but Brightly's cave was fairly dry and quite sheltered. He had built up the entrance with shaped stones taken from the long-abandoned copper-mines below. The cleft was full of copper, which stained the water a delightful shade of green.

18  The dealer in rabbit-skins was not alone in the world. He had a dog, which was rubbish like its master. The animal was of no recognised breed, although in a dim light it called itself a fox-terrier. She could not have been an intelligent dog, or she would not have remained constant to Brightly. Her name was Ju, which was an abbreviation of Jerusalem. One Sunday evening Brightly had slipped inside a church, and somewhat to his surprise had been allowed to remain, although an usher was told to keep an eye upon him and see that he did not break open the empty poor-box. A hymn was sung about Jerusalem the golden, where happy souls were indulging in over-eating themselves in a sort of glorified dairy filled with milk and honey. The hymn enraptured Brightly, who was, of course, tired and famished; and when he had left the warm church, although without any of the promised milk and honey, he kept on murmuring the lines and trying to recall the music. He could think of nothing but Jerusalem for some days. He went into the public library at Tavistock and looked it up in a map of the world, discovered it was in a country called Palestine, and wondered how many rabbit-skins it would cost to take him there. Brightly reckoned in rabbit-skins, not in shillings and pence, which were matters he was not very familiar with. He noticed that whenever he mentioned the name of Jerusalem the dog wagged her tail, as though she too was interested in the dairy produce; so, as the animal lacked a title, Jerusalem was awarded her. Brightly thought of the milk and honey whenever he called his poor half-starved dog. Nobody wanted Brightly, because he was not of the least importance. He hadn't got a vote, or any of those things which make the world desire the presence of people.

38  Presently he thought he had coughed long enough, so he picked up his basket and went on climbing the road, his body bent as usual towards the right. At a distance he looked like the half of a circle. He could not stand straight. The weight of his basket and habit had crooked him like an oak branch. He tramped on towards the barren village of St. Mary Tavy. There

was a certain amount of wild scenery to be admired. Away to the right was Brentor and the church upon its crags. To the left were piled the rocks of the abandoned copper-mines. The name of Wheal Friendship might have had a cheerful sound for Brightly had he known what friendship meant. He didn't look at the scenery, because he was half blind. He could see his way about, but that was all. He lived in the twilight.

47 Brightly did not think much while he tramped the moor. He had no right to think. It was not in the way of business. Still, he had his dream, not more than one, because he was not troubled with an active imagination. He tried to fancy himself going about, not on his tired rheumatic legs, but in a little cart, with fern at the bottom for Ju to lie on, and a bit of board at the side bearing in white letters the inscription: "A. Brightly. Purveyor of rabbit-skins"; and a lamp to be lighted after dark, and a plank for himself to sit on. All this splendour to be drawn by a little shaggy pony. What a great man he would be in those days!

*gorges – narrow valleys between mountains or hills

*cleft – a split in the ground.

Answer all questions in Section A.

**01**   Read again the first part of the source, from **lines 1-7**.

List **four** things about Brightly from this part of the source.      **[4 marks]**

**02**   Look in detail at this extract, from **lines 8 to 17** of the source.

> Brightly had a home. The river saw to that; not the Tavy, but the less romantic Taw. On the Western side of Cawsand are many gorges in the great cleft cut by the Taw between Belstone and Sticklepath. There narrow and deep clefts have been made by the persistent water draining down to the Taw from the bogs above. In the largest of these clefts Brightly was at home. The sides were completely hidden by willow-scrub, immense ferns, and clumps of whortleberries, as well as by overhanging masses of granite. The water could be heard dripping below like a chime of fairy bells. In winter the cleft appeared a white cascade of falling water, but Brightly's cave was fairly dry and quite sheltered. He had built up the entrance with shaped stones taken from the long-abandoned copper-mines below. The cleft was full of copper, which stained the water a delightful shade of green.

How does the writer use language here to describe the setting?

You could include the writer's choice of:

- Words and phrases
- Language features and techniques
- Sentence forms.                                              **[8 marks]**

**03**   You now need to think about the **whole** of the source.

This text is from the beginning of a short story.

How has the writer structured the text to interest you as a reader?

You could write about:

- What the writer focuses your attention on at the beginning of the source
- How and why the writer changes this focus as the source develops

- Any other structural features that interest you. **[8 marks]**

**04**

Focus this part of your answer on the second part of the source, from **line 18 to the end**.

A reader said, 'When Brightly is in the church, he enjoys his time there, and it has a positive effect on him, even though his life is hard.'

To what extent do you agree?

In your response, you could:
- Consider your own impressions of Brightly
- Evaluate how the writer has created these impressions
- Support your response with references to the text. **[20 marks]**

# Section B: Writing

**05**

A travel website is running a creative writing competition.

**Either**

Describe a journey, as suggested by this picture:

**or**

Write a story with the title 'The Holiday'

(24 marks for content and organisation
16 marks for technical accuracy)
**[40 marks]**

Printed in Great Britain
by Amazon